Handwriting Without Tears®

Kindergarten
Teacher's Guide

Guide to Multisensory Lessons
and Activities for...

Handwriting Without Tears®

Name:

Print Child's Name

Letters and Numbers for Me

cow   dog   kite   queen

by Jan Z. Olsen, OTR and Emily F. Knapton, M.Ed., OTR/L

Handwriting Without Tears®

8001 MacArthur Blvd
Cabin John, MD 20818
301.263.2700
www.hwtears.com

Authors: Jan Z. Olsen, OTR and Emily F. Knapton, M.Ed., OTR/L
Illustrator: Jan Z. Olsen, OTR
HWT Editors: Annie Cassidy and Jen Girdish
HWT Graphic Designer: Julie Koborg

How can I access the online resources in this guide?

To make these resources available to you, we created a password protected section of our website exclusively for those who have a teacher's guide. There you will find instructional resources, school-to-home connections, new tips, and additional handwriting activities to share with students, families, and other educators.

Just go to **hwtears.com/click** and enter the **passcode** printed on the back cover of this guide.

Welcome

Welcome to Handwriting Without Tears® and to teaching handwriting in kindergarten.

This is your teacher's guide, not only for the student workbook, but for a way of teaching handwriting that is effective for children. Your kindergarteners will be moving, singing, and playing with you as they build and write letters. That's how good handwriting starts—with hands-on materials and teaching that bring the curriculum to life.

Explicit, multisensory handwriting instruction in kindergarten is crucial. This is the year to actively and joyfully teach handwriting habits. Good habits lead to good handwriting and that directly links to literacy and overall school success (Lust and Donica 2011).

Handwriting Without Tears started in the 1970s and has evolved based on our continued and direct experience with students, teachers, occupational therapists, and administrators around the country. Our 35 years of experience and ongoing collaboration solve the problems associated with teaching handwriting and do so in a way that is joyful, effective, and innovative.

Our materials and teaching strategies make learning a positive, successful experience for children in just 15 minutes a day. You will help your students build strong printing skills for writing letters, words, and sentences. Every lesson includes a multisensory element and has additional, optional connections to tie handwriting to other parts of your school day.

We support teacher directed learning. We believe you'll enjoy using our program and are excited to have you bring the program to life in your classroom.

Emily F. Knapton   Jan Z. Olsen

A B C D E F G H I J K L M N O P Q R S T U V W X Y Z

94 73 88 71 70 69 91 78 95 97 79 80 76 75 89 72 90 74 93 96 81 82 83 84 85 86

a b c d e f g h i j k l m n o p q r s t u v w x y z

101 - Lowercase Letters,
Words, Sentences & More

157 - Numbers

173 - Resources

Get to Know Handwriting Without Tears®

Our Philosophy

Children's handwriting matters. It matters now, next year, and for years to come. Handwriting skills affect school success (Feder and Majnemer 2007). With our easy-to-teach, easy-to-learn curriculum, you will be empowered to teach handwriting efficiently and well. With your guidance, children will learn correct letter formation and good handwriting habits that will serve them well in every subject.

Handwriting instruction, in the past, was viewed as a "core" skill that teachers were taught to teach. Over time, university teaching programs moved away from the emphasis of handwriting. The result has deprived today's teachers—and students—of a valuable and necessary skill.

Handwriting is a skill that must be taught. We teach it deliberately and systematically because we want children to write with good habits automatically. This skill mastery frees children to focus on the content of their writing, instead of the mechanics.

Elementary students spend the majority of their day doing handwriting work, and good handwriting skills help students write with speed and ease in all their subjects. The earlier children master this skill, the more likely they are to succeed in school.

The Handwriting Without Tears curriculum draws from years of innovation and research to provide developmentally appropriate, multisensory tools and strategies for your classroom. The program follows research that demonstrates children learn more effectively by actively doing, with materials that address all styles of learning.

We teach effectively with joy. We have figured out easier, happier ways for children to master handwriting. Handwriting Without Tears is dedicated to developing excellent materials for children and training for teachers. As a result, millions of administrators, teachers, therapists, parents, and children across the country have successfully used our program. The result truly is handwriting without tears!

Principles of Effective Curriculum Design

To most effectively help children, our curriculum follows three principles.

1. Simply Smart Student Materials

We design all our materials to be intuitive, engaging, and developmentally progressive. We've used our direct experience and knowledge of how students learn the best to develop unique teaching materials that are easy and fun.

2. Active Teaching

We facilitate instruction that engages children, so that they are active participants. You and the students will move, sing, talk, and experience the lessons. You will immediately know the effect of the instruction and can adjust, repeat, or vary the instruction for the best learning outcome.

3. Teacher Support

We believe that if you have knowledge of handwriting and the latest advances in the field, you will be empowered. We can answer your handwriting questions and help you with your concerns. Why are children mixing up capitals and lowercase? What about reversals? We provide answers to understand and avoid those problems.

Simply Smart Student Materials

Workbook Design

We carefully plan every workbook page and everything that's on it. Our workbooks are accessible and friendly, yet also promote excellence. We want children to practice correctly, therefore our workbook pages promote efficient, effective practice for each letter.

Child Friendly, Simple Language

Our child friendly language evolved in response to complicated letter formation terminology in other programs. When teaching letter formation, we eliminate language that assumes that children understand left/right orientation, clockwise/counter-clockwise, or forward/backward circles. We make it easy by using fewer, carefully selected words that all children know and understand.

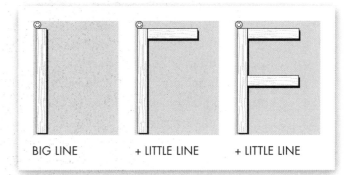

BIG LINE   + LITTLE LINE   + LITTLE LINE

Large Step-by-Step Models

It is much easier for children to understand how to form letters if you show them how step by step. Our workbooks contain large step-by-step images that show students how to make each part of every letter.

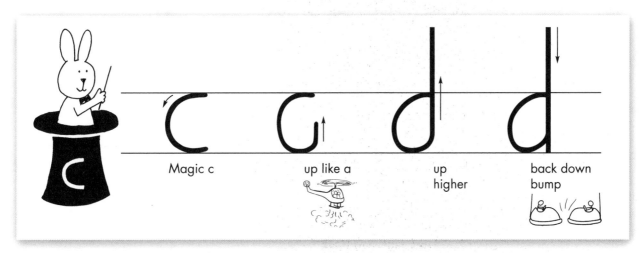

Magic c   up like a   up higher   back down bump

Our workbooks are lefty friendly. Teaching pages provide models on the left and right so that left-handed children can easily see the model they are copying. Lefties never have to lift their hands or place them in an awkward position to see a model. Children always make their best letter directly beside a model. This design encourages excellent letter practice for both left- and right-handed children.

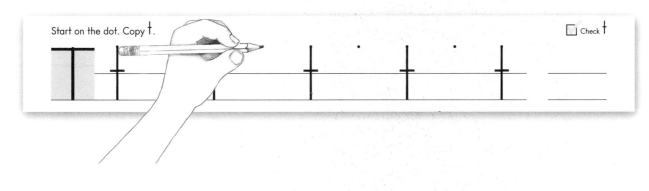

Start on the dot. Copy †.   ☐ Check †

Simply Smart Student Materials

Developmental Teaching Order

Teaching in a developmental order helps children master skills and boosts confidence. We teach the easiest skills first, then build on prior knowledge (p. 52). Capitals are taught first, and lowercase letters follow. All letters are taught in small groups of similar formation (pp. 67 and 102). Our teaching sequence takes advantage of child development and brain research to promote effective learning and good habits.

Black & White, Simple, Clean Design & Illustrations

The black and white pages in our workbooks are clean and clear. We deliberately avoid visually confusing backgrounds, colored graphics, crowded pages, and multicolored lines. These fancy effects are overdone and distracting to teaching. They create visual perception difficulties for children. Our simple workbook pages are appealing and invite children to color and draw once they have finished the lesson.

Our illustrations promote left-to-right directionality. This is a unique feature of our workbooks. The car, helicopter, horse, and other drawings move left to right across the page to encourage correct visual tracking and writing direction.

Words with Familiar Letters

Every word we teach is carefully chosen. We want children to practice new letters only with familiar, already taught letters. This practice builds skill and confidence without the frustration of writing words with letters they haven't learned.

Continuous, Meaningful Review

Children retain skills better if they have continuous, meaningful review. That's why each new letter is used in words and sentences that emphasize practice of the new letter and help children review and practice previously learned letters.

Cross-Curricular Connections

In addition to handwriting, we want the pages to have connections to other grade-appropriate curricula. Whenever possible, we integrate Common Core State Standards and grade-appropriate skills in our teaching. We create pages that help you teach handwriting, and review other grade-appropriate skills.

Simple Spatial Organization

We begin by teaching capital letters and numbers with Gray Blocks. The Gray Blocks prevent reversals and help children learn how to place letters and numbers. Our simple letter and number teaching strategies produce letters and numbers that are reversal-proof.

As children move to lowercase, our double lines foster handwriting success. The mid line is for size. The base line is for placement. Small letters fit in the middle space. Tall letters go in the top space. Descending letters go in the bottom space. Double lines make it easy for children to place letters and to make them the right size.

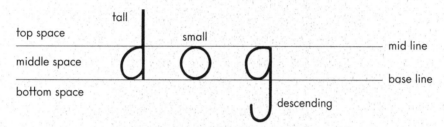

When children are learning to print, they need extra room to write. Many workbooks and worksheets are poorly designed, requiring students to cram their words to fit into spaces that are too small. Our landscape style workbooks give them the space they need to write and develop good spacing habits.

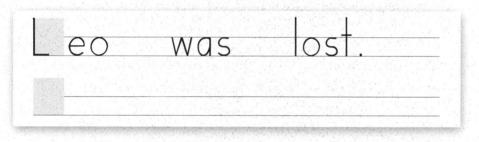

Line Generalization: Success on All Paper Styles

Our workbooks provide activities for children to experience different types of lined paper. They begin with the simple double lines, then we teach them to master all lines.

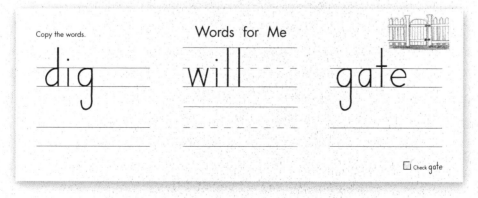

Simply Smart Student Materials

About the Kindergarten Curriculum

This curriculum fits easily into your daily kindergarten routine. As you become familiar with the program, you will gradually incorporate new activities and choose those that suit your students' needs. Here's how:

Building

Children love to build things. They will enjoy building capital letters and numbers. These materials help organize children by teaching them letter formation and orientation.

Wood Pieces Set for Capitals Letters, Capital Letter Cards & Mat for Wood Pieces

Included are the four basic shapes used to build capital letters: eight Big Lines, six Little Lines, six Big Curves, six Little Curves.

Children polish, sort, stack, and learn the names of the Wood Pieces. When they use Wood Pieces in teacher-directed play, they learn size, shape, and position concepts. Whey they're ready for letters, they use the Wood Pieces to build letters. For example: they make **B** with a Big Line + Little Curve + Little Curve. The Mat and Letter Cards use a ☺ as an orientation icon on the top left corner.

Music & Movement

You sing to and with children. There are songs for tapping Big Lines and writing letters in the air. Children love to participate and follow your lead. For some, music unlocks language. That's why we created the *Rock, Rap, Tap & Learn* CD.

***Rock, Rap, Tap & Learn* CD**

Use the CD to make learning letters and numbers fun and memorable. Music promotes movement. Whether you are teaching descending letters or spacing skills, this CD will charge up your lessons and catch your students' attention.

Imaginary Play

Funny voices and props captivate children. We believe in dynamic teaching to make it fun and more effective.

Magic C Bunny

Make the puppet your teaching assistant. Your students can use him, too. See p. 188 for directions to make your own Magic C Bunny out of a paper napkin. Your students will form letters correctly when they learn the Magic C way.

Pre-Writing Capitals, Numbers & Lowercase

Children have many different learning styles. That's why pre-writing activities using multisensory materials can make learning easy and fun. To help children form letters before paper and pencil, have children trace large models with Little Chalk Bits and Little Sponge Cubes to build good habits.

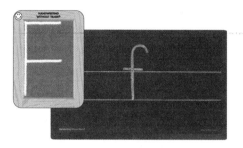

Slate Chalkboard & Blackboard with Double Lines

Use the Slate Chalkboard to teach capitals and numbers. The Blackboard with Double Lines is used to teach lowercase letters. Incorporate our Wet-Dry-Try technique to add endless opportunities to trace, write, and learn to form letters and numbers.

Writing Letters, Numbers, Words & Sentences

After pre-writing, children are ready for a more formal approach to handwriting. Our workbooks are carefully designed to teach letters and numbers in a developmental sequence.

Letters and Numbers for Me workbook

Follow the lessons in the workbook. It's loaded with capital, lowercase, word, sentence, and number practice. Your students will love the fun activities, which develop their handwriting and sentence skills. We have developed 36 weeks of teaching guidelines in this teacher's guide (p. 175) to help you plan your lessons.

Promoting Good Pencil Grip Use through Coloring, Drawing & Writing

If we want children to hold their pencils correctly, we have to explicitly teach them a proper grip and provide them with tools that are the right size for their hands. At Handwriting Without Tears® we believe in little tools for little hands.

FLIP Crayons®

Use FLIP Crayons to help children develop hand coordination and fine motor skills. They will love flipping them over and over to change colors.

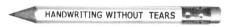

Pencils for Little Hands

Use golf-size pencils with kindergarten children. Let them write with pencils that fit their hand size.

Simply Smart Student Materials

Using *Letters and Numbers for Me* workbook

Letters and Numbers for Me is divided into three major sections—capitals, lowercase letters, and numbers. You will also find Words for Me and Sentences for Me activities. These pages give children the opportunity to practice their new letters in fun language arts activities that are age appropriate.

Capital Letter & Word Pages

Our capital letter pages show large step-by-step instructions for letter formation with Wood Pieces and on the Slate Chalkboard. The ☑ teaches children to self-check their work. Capital letters are reinforced with real world examples of capitals and practice on Gray Blocks to prevent reversals.

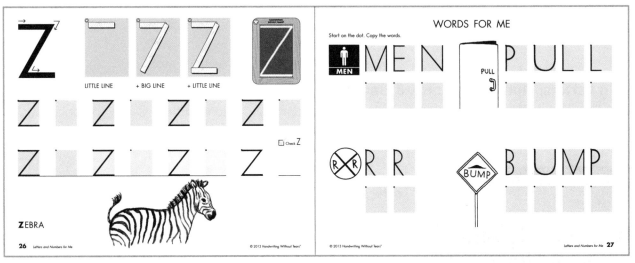

Capital Letter Lesson   Word Lesson

Lowercase Letter, Word & Sentence Pages

These pages use newly taught letters to practice words and sentences. They also model good spacing and review capitals. The ☑ teaches children self-checking to reinforce letter formation and sentence skills.

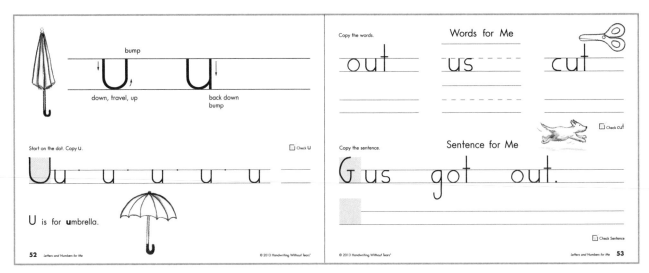

Lowercase Letter Lessons   Words & Sentence Lesson

Activity & Language Arts Pages

Language arts pages are fun and engaging for students, promoting meaningful practice. We designed these pages to help children learn to write words, poems, and paragraphs.

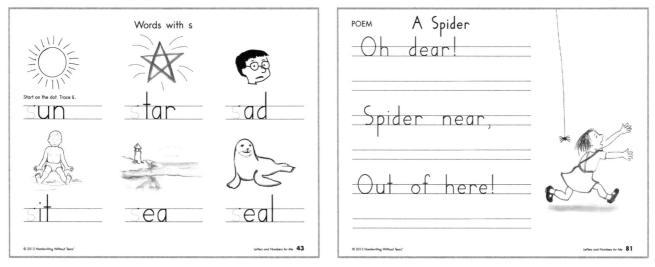

Activity Page

Language Arts Lesson

Number Pages

On our number pages, we teach numbers in Gray Blocks to prevent reversals. We also use fun stories to accompany step-by-step number instruction. Review pages provide formation and counting practice.

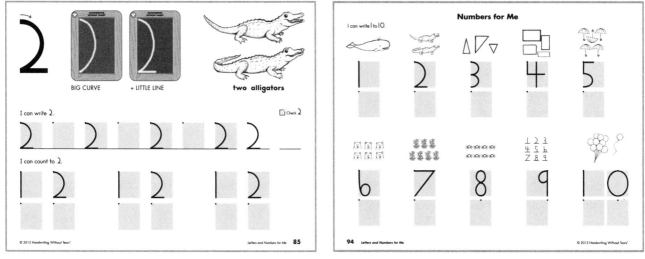

Number Lesson

Number Lesson

Active Teaching

Kindergarten Teacher's Guide: What You'll Find and How to Use It

This teacher's guide was designed to help you create a learning environment where your students are engaged, active participants. The sections are developmentally sequenced and paced to let children master each skill before proceeding to the next. Each section has a mix of hands-on activities and letter lessons. The lessons contain a variety of ways to teach as well as options to support or repeat instruction for the best outcomes.

Foundation Skills (p. 23)

At the start of school year, we introduce accessible activities that every child can do, activities that prepare every child to do well! Children learn to shake hands and say hello. They play with Wood Pieces and learn to sort and name "Big Lines and Little Lines, Big Curves and Little Curves." Later, they'll understand you when you say **D** has one Big Line and one Big Curve. By showing children how to sit, place the paper, and hold the pencil, you build readiness! It's fun, effective, and develops the foundation for successful writing.

Writing Capitals (p. 51)

We teach the capital letters as a group, separate from the lowercase letters. We introduce capitals with multisensory, hands-on lessons. This makes an easy transition from building letters to writing in the workbook. In every lesson, you model letter formation for your students. Show them how to start at the top and how to make every stroke in the right sequence. Week after week, children develop handwriting skills with hands-on letter and workbook lessons.

Lowercase Letters, Words, Sentences & More (p. 101)

Lowercase lessons begin with letters your students already know. We start with **c**, **o**, **s**, **v**, **w**—five letters that are exactly the same as capitals, just smaller. Each letter or letter group has its own activities, songs, stories, or movement. As they learn lowercase letters, they practice letters they know in words and sentences. With letter, word, and sentence skills well in hand, we introduce children to fuller written expression with activity pages.

Numbers (p. 157)

Numbers may be at the back of the teacher's guide, but like capitals, they are taught at the beginning of the year. Teach numbers during your math lessons. We suggest two numbers per week, but a slower pace would be fine. Bring out the Slate Chalkboards, chalk, sponges, and paper towels. You'll need those materials to teach numbers with Wet-Dry-Try. This is multisensory instruction at its best and a delightful, effective way to teach numbers.

Connections (throughout)

At the bottom of each lesson, you will find a Connections section. This section helps to connect the lesson to another subject, technology, or provides a Home Link.

Resources (p. 173)

In the back of the book are important resources to support your teaching throughout the year and help you guide, adjust, and monitor your instruction.

- Teaching Guidelines
- Remediation Tips
- School-to-Home Connections
- Handwriting Standards for Kindergarten
- Common Core State Standards
- Letter Chart

Activity Design

You'll be teaching with a combination of multisensory activities and workbook lessons. This guide includes plans for both activities and workbook pages. Below is an example of an activity plan. On the next page is a letter lesson plan.

Information – Brief explanation of the activity and its purpose.

Activity – The main activity is described in simple steps. Bold type shows what to say.

A Click Away – A smiley face icon means you will find additional instructional resources, school-to-home connections, new tips, and additional handwriting activities online.

Support/ELL – Suggestions for modifying or reinforcing the activity.

Check – Ways to assess children's response/learning and to tell if activity is being used correctly.

More to Learn – Ways to extend learning by adding complexity or variety.

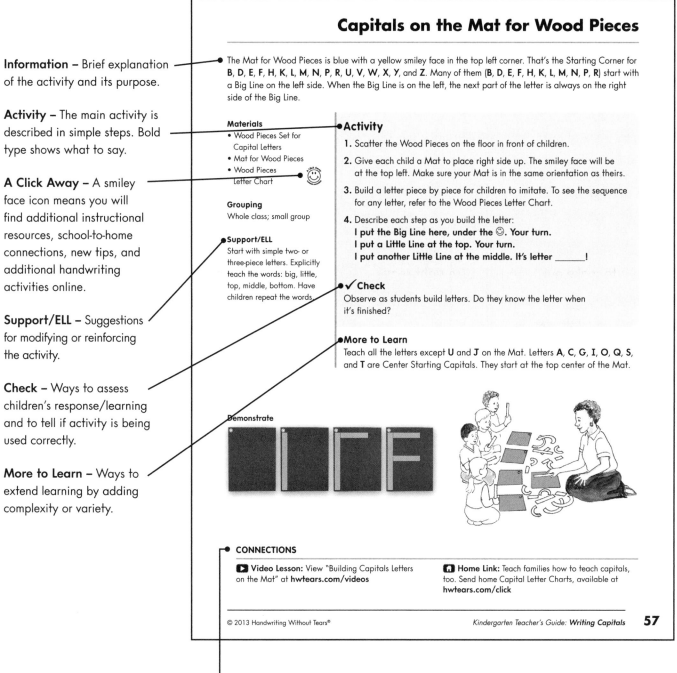

Capitals on the Mat for Wood Pieces

The Mat for Wood Pieces is blue with a yellow smiley face in the top left corner. That's the Starting Corner for **B, D, E, F, H, K, L, M, N, P, R, U, V, W, X, Y,** and **Z.** Many of them (**B, D, E, F, H, K, L, M, N, P, R**) start with a Big Line on the left side. When the Big Line is on the left, the next part of the letter is always on the right side of the Big Line.

Materials
• Wood Pieces Set for Capital Letters
• Mat for Wood Pieces
• Wood Pieces Letter Chart

Grouping
Whole class; small group

Support/ELL
Start with simple two- or three-piece letters. Explicitly teach the words: big, little, top, middle, bottom. Have children repeat the words.

Activity

1. Scatter the Wood Pieces on the floor in front of children.

2. Give each child a Mat to place right side up. The smiley face will be at the top left. Make sure your Mat is in the same orientation as theirs.

3. Build a letter piece by piece for children to imitate. To see the sequence for any letter, refer to the Wood Pieces Letter Chart.

4. Describe each step as you build the letter:
   I put the Big Line here, under the ☺. Your turn.
   I put a Little Line at the top. Your turn.
   I put another Little Line at the middle. It's letter _____!

✓ Check
Observe as students build letters. Do they know the letter when it's finished?

More to Learn
Teach all the letters except **U** and **J** on the Mat. Letters **A, C, G, I, O, Q, S,** and **T** are Center Starting Capitals. They start at the top center of the Mat.

Demonstrate

CONNECTIONS

▶ **Video Lesson:** View "Building Capitals Letters on the Mat" at **hwtears.com/videos**

🏠 **Home Link:** Teach families how to teach capitals, too. Send home Capital Letter Charts, available at **hwtears.com/click**

© 2013 Handwriting Without Tears®   *Kindergarten Teacher's Guide: **Writing Capitals*** **57**

Connections – This section helps to connect the activity to another subject, technology, or a Home Link.

Active Teaching

Letter Lesson Design

Active teaching and demonstration bring workbook lessons to life. This guide has lesson plans and strategies for every workbook page. Below is an example of a letter lesson plan.

Letter Lesson Heading – Letter is shown prominently in the top corner. Features language for teaching the letter.

Lesson Plan – The letter lesson follows these steps:

Introduce the letter and the page.

Demonstrate – Children finger trace while you demonstrate letter formation. Children then copy the letter.

Copy – Children watch you model the word and then copy it.

Check & Evaluate – Children check their letter and evaluate their formation.

Read, Color & Draw – You and children read the sentence. Children color and draw.

More to Learn – Ways to extend learning by adding complexity or variety.

Support/ELL – Suggestions for modifying or simplifying the activity.

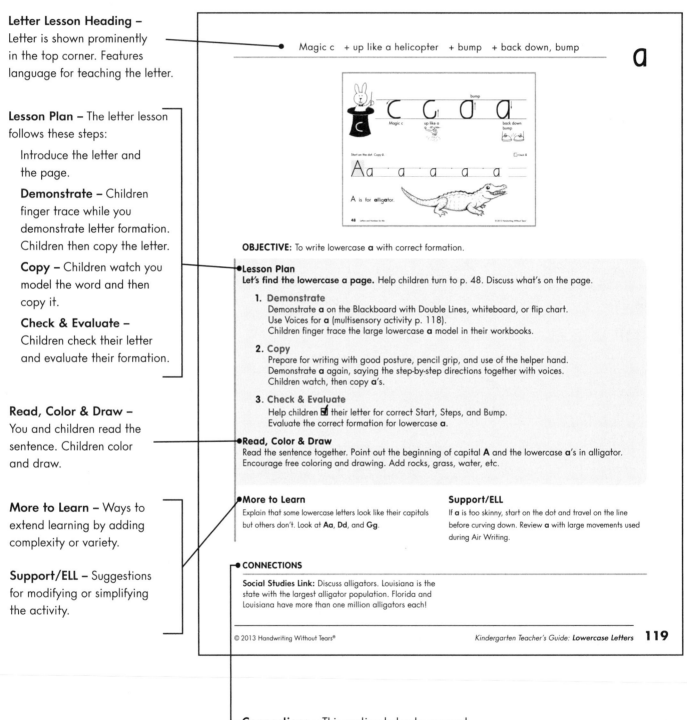

Magic c + up like a helicopter + bump + back down, bump

OBJECTIVE: To write lowercase **a** with correct formation.

Lesson Plan
Let's find the lowercase a page. Help children turn to p. 48. Discuss what's on the page.

1. **Demonstrate**
Demonstrate **a** on the Blackboard with Double Lines, whiteboard, or flip chart.
Use Voices for **a** (multisensory activity p. 118).
Children finger trace the large lowercase **a** model in their workbooks.

2. **Copy**
Prepare for writing with good posture, pencil grip, and use of the helper hand.
Demonstrate **a** again, saying the step-by-step directions together with voices.
Children watch, then copy **a**'s.

3. **Check & Evaluate**
Help children ☑ their letter for correct Start, Steps, and Bump.
Evaluate the correct formation for lowercase **a**.

Read, Color & Draw
Read the sentence together. Point out the beginning of capital **A** and the lowercase **a**'s in alligator. Encourage free coloring and drawing. Add rocks, grass, water, etc.

More to Learn
Explain that some lowercase letters look like their capitals but others don't. Look at **Aa**, **Dd**, and **Gg**.

Support/ELL
If **a** is too skinny, start on the dot and travel on the line before curving down. Review **a** with large movements used during Air Writing.

CONNECTIONS

Social Studies Link: Discuss alligators. Louisiana is the state with the largest alligator population. Florida and Louisiana have more than one million alligators each!

Kindergarten Teacher's Guide: Lowercase Letters **119**

Connections – This section helps to connect the lesson to another subject, technology, or a Home Link.

Explicit Demonstration & Multisensory Instruction

Children need explicit letter formation demonstration to achieve legible and fluent handwriting. Providing students with structured handwriting lessons leads to improved writing performance. Our lessons demonstrate step-by-step formation, to help children develop correct letter formation habits.

Activities with hands-on materials address different senses to teach correct formation, spacing, and sequencing. We help children develop their writing skills through explicit, multisensory, play-based instruction. Children move, touch, feel, and manipulate real objects as they learn the habits and skills essential for writing. Music makes learning fun and is integral to how children learn. We use music to speak to children and promote movement and memory.

As a kindergarten teacher, you know the importance of self-directed play and multisensory, active learning. Research is on your side. It supports multisensory teaching to address children's diverse learning styles: visual, tactile, auditory, and kinesthetic.

Visual
- Illustrations of letter formation give clear, step-by-step visual direction.
- Pages are black and white, appealing, and uncluttered.
- Illustrations in workbooks promote left-to-right visual tracking and writing.
- Smiley face orients children to the top.

Tactile
- Workbook models are big enough for finger tracing.
- Wet-Dry-Try (pp. 59, 105, and 159) gives children touch and repitition without boredom.
- The frame of the Slate Chalkboard helps children make lines and avoid reversals.

Auditory
- Language is consistent and child friendly to help children easily learn and remember.
- CD's use the power of music to facilitate participation, memory, and joyful learning.
- Lessons are engaging with active teaching and student participation.

Kinesthetic
- Music and movement teach letter formation.
- Air Writing (p. 61) and Door Tracing (p. 64) teach using large arm movements and visual cues.
- Digital Teaching Tools teach letter formation on an interactive whiteboard.

You can facilitate multisensory experiences if you:
- Use the ☺ to orient children to the top
- Are dynamic and joyful
- Vary the multisensory lessons you use

Teacher Support

The essentials of kindergarten handwriting instruction are in this teacher's guide, but you will find additional support through our resource materials and through our superbly productive and fun workshops.

Teaching Guidelines

Teaching guidelines help you plan your days. We've provided a suggested roadmap to complete the workbook in 22 weeks. In addition, we've included 14 additional weeks of suggested activities for functional writing practice. Lessons are easy and need little prep time to teach handwriting effectively in only 15 minutes per day.

A Click Away

Throughout this teacher's guide you will see the smiley face icon ☺ to visit A Click Away. This password-protected site is a great resource exclusively for teacher's guide users. You will find downloads to supplement your handwriting instruction or to send home to families to foster a school-to-home connection.

Enliven your classroom and help your students master handwriting with ease. Browse through our continually expanding collection of downloads. You'll find plenty of activities and support materials. These online resources are great supplements for your teacher's guide.

For kindergarten, you will find Pencil Pick-Ups, music activities, lyrics, Home Link downloads, and other activities with active learning opportunities.

☺ Visit **hwtears.com/click** to register with the passcode on the back cover of this teacher's guide.

Home Links

We have provided Home Links at the bottom of lessons that can be extended to the home. These downloads can be sent home to families to foster a positive school-to-home connection and promote learning outside the classroom.

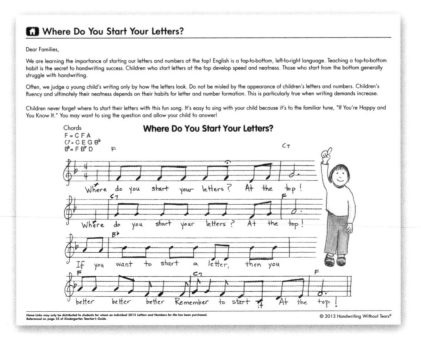

Assessments

It's helpful for you to gather information about the children in your room so you understand their experiences entering kindergarten. We have Pre-K assessments that can inform and guide your instruction in the beginning of the year. Download these assessments at **hwtears.com/checkreadiness**

We also created the Screener of Handwriting Proficiency. This unique handwriting screening tool helps you track individual and class progress throughout the year. It's also an adaptive assessment, providing recommendations for remediation by child. Use the Screener in an RtI model or to help identify struggling students. Visit **hwtears.com/screener** to register.

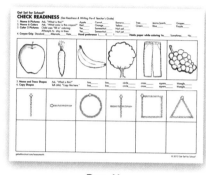

Pre-K:
Readiness & Writing Assessment

Kindergarten:
Screener of Handwriting Proficiency

Differentiated Instruction

We provide multiple avenues for teaching each lesson to mesh with individual students' interests, abilities, and learning styles.

Remediation Tips

We have dedicated a section of this teacher's guide for evaluation and remediation tips. These strategies can help you correct handwriting difficulties and modify the curriculum to meet the needs of your students.

English Language Learner (ELL) Strategies

We developed our curriculum to meet the needs of all learners, including English language learners. We employ a variety of research based teaching strategies to help diverse learners master handwriting. These embedded strategies provide simple best practices that can be seamlessly integrated into a classroom setting and that benefit all children.

Our curriculum addresses the necessary components needed for success in an ELL classroom, including:

• Prior Knowledge Activation
• Conducive and Cooperative Learning Environment
• Multisensory, Thematic Instruction
• Repeated Lesson/Concept/Vocabulary
• Immediate Feedback and Think-Aloud Modeling

Visit **hwtears.com/click** to download printing strategies for English language learners and how Handwriting Without Tears® can be integrated in an ELL classroom.

Teacher Support

Technology & Handwriting

Introduce our simple technology into your daily classroom experience and make learning letters more engaging and fun. Our offerings expose children to the world of technology in an appropriate manner. Whether you are using technology with your class or developing worksheets for spelling, vocabulary, or practice writing, technology can support your handwriting instruction.

Digital Teaching Tools

Engage your students with our Digital Teaching Tools. We are delighted to offer this technology to teach to different learning styles and to make A+ worksheets. It's a new way for you to demonstrate letter and number formations and teach different learning styles. Visit **hwtears.com/dtt**

Letter & Number Formations

Now, you can model the steps for printing lowercase letters, capitals, and numbers using an interactive whiteboard, or any computer with Adobe Flash capabilities. Children follow along by using big arm movements or by finger tracing the steps using the same consistent, child friendly language found in our workbooks.

Features:
- Letter formations
- Number formations
- Child friendly terminology
- Spanish characters

A+ Worksheet Maker

The Handwriting Without Tears® A+ Worksheet Maker is an easy-to-use classroom resource that enables you to integrate the unique Handwriting Without Tears font and double lines into other classroom activities.

Features:
- Models to facilitate good handwriting practice
- Kindergarten-level appropriate lines and adequate spacing
- Spelling, sentence, and vocabulary worksheet templates

Screener of Handwriting Proficiency

The Screener of Handwriting Proficiency is a one-of-a-kind, free, easy-to-administer, whole class assessment that helps you identify students and classes that are struggling with handwriting. Teachers and occupational therapists can use the Screener to identify and measure specific skill areas where students need print instruction and intervention throughout the year. The Screener is universal and can be used independently or as part of an RtI framework. Visit **hwtears.com/screener**

Video Lessons

If you are a visual learner or want to see the lessons in action, we have a robust video library of many of our activities and lessons in this teacher's guide. Watch teachers and occupational therapists using materials with students. Many lessons have a video link under Connections. For a complete list of video lessons, go to **hwtears.com/videos**

Online Seminars

Join us for interactive exchanges with program experts and other education professionals. For more information, visit **hwtears.com/webinars**

E-Newsletters

Receive free tips, resources, engaging articles, activities, and free downloads when you sign up for our newsletters. They are designed to help you get the most out of teaching our program. To register for one or all of our e-newsletters, visit **hwtears.com/newsletters**

Professional Development

We are nationally recognized for our outstanding and engaging professional development workshops and continuing education opportunities. Educators benefit from the extensive support we offer. We present hundreds of handwriting workshops every year across the United States and Canada. Our Handwriting Workshop uses a fun, hands-on approach to dynamic instruction in the teaching methodology from kindergarten through fifth grade.

Our Get Set for School® Pre-K Workshops introduce a writing readiness, literacy, and math curriculum full of developmentally appropriate activities that teach children about letters, body awareness, numbers, sequencing, and sharing in a fun and engaging manner.

The Print Tool® Workshop will provide all the training necessary to evaluate any child in printing and provide a detailed remediation plan. All workshops include strategies and materials to use immediately in the classroom.

Scope & Sequence of Printing

The Scope & Sequence of Printing defines the content and order of printing instruction. The skills needed for printing develop as early as Pre-K. Although we do not teach printing formally at the Pre-K level, we can create an environment and encourage activities to develop good habits that students need in kindergarten. The secret is teaching skills in a way that makes learning natural, easy, and fun.

Type of Instruction

Informal/Structured: A variety of activities address the broad range of letter and school readiness skills.

Formal/Structured: Teacher-directed activities are presented in a more precise order with specific objectives.

Handwriting Sequence

Pre-Strokes: These are beginning marks that can be random or deliberate.

Shapes: These are often introduced before letters and are a foundation for letter formation skills.

Capitals/Numbers: These use simple shapes and strokes. They have the same size, start, and position.

Lowercase Letters: These are tall, small, and descending symbols with more complex strokes, sizes, starts, and positions.

Stages of Learning

Pre-Instruction Readiness: Attention, behavior, language, and fine motor skills for beginning writing.

Stage 1–Imitating the Teacher: Watch someone form a letter first, and then write it.

Stage 2–Copying Printed Models: Look at a letter and then write it.

Stage 3–Independent Writing: Write without watching someone or even seeing a letter.

Physical Approach

Crayon Use: Crayons prepare children to use pencils. Small crayon use encourages proper grip.

Pencil Use: Proper pencil grip facilitates good handwriting. In kindergarten, children transfer their crayon grip to pencils.

Posture: Good sitting posture promotes good handwriting. This is taught in kindergarten.

Paper Placement: Correct paper placement helps children move the writing hand across the page. Paper placement is different for left- and right-handed children.

Printing Skills

Primary Skills
 – Memory: Remember and write dictated letters and numbers.
 – Orientation: Face letters and numbers in the correct direction.
 – Start: Begin each letter or number correctly.
 – Sequence: Make the letter strokes in the correct order.

Secondary Skills
 – Placement: Place letters and numbers on the base line.
 – Size: Write in a consistent, grade-appropriate size.
 – Spacing: Place letters in words close, put space between words.
 – Control: Focus on neatness and proportion.

Functional Writing

Letters/Numbers, Words, Sentences, Paragraphs, and Writing in All Subjects

SCOPE & SEQUENCE OF PRINTING

	Pre-K	Kindergarten	1st Grade	2nd Grade
Type of Instruction				
Informal/Structured	✓			
Formal/Structured		✓	✓	✓
Handwriting Sequence				
Pre-Strokes	✓			
Shapes	✓			
Capitals/Numbers	✓	✓	✓	✓
Lowercase Letters	*See note below	✓	✓	✓
Stages of Learning				
Pre-Instruction Readiness	✓	✓		
Stage 1–Imitating the Teacher	✓	✓	✓	✓
Stage 2–Copying Printed Models		✓	✓	✓
Stage 3–Independent Writing		✓	✓	✓
Physical Approach				
Crayon Use	✓	✓		
Pencil Use		✓	✓	✓
Posture		✓	✓	✓
Paper Placement		✓	✓	✓
Printing Skills				
Primary Skills				
– Memory	✓	✓	✓	✓
– Orientation	✓	✓	✓	✓
– Start	✓	✓	✓	✓
– Sequence	✓	✓	✓	✓
Secondary Skills				
– Placement		✓	✓	✓
– Size		✓	✓	✓
– Spacing		✓	✓	✓
– Control		✓ Emerging	✓	✓
Functional Writing				
Letters/Numbers	✓ Capitals/Numbers	✓	✓	
Words		✓ Short	✓ Short	✓ Long
Sentences		✓ Short	✓ Short	✓ Long
Paragraphs			✓ Short	✓ Long
Writing in All Subjects		✓	✓	✓

*Children in Pre-K are taught lowercase letter recognition, but not writing. They may be taught how to write the lowercase letters in their names.

FOUNDATION SKILLS

Letters and numbers are the foundation of literacy. Kindergarten teachers not only teach them, they teach children how to use them for reading, writing, and math. The success of kindergarten instruction depends on readiness skills.

To make sure children are ready to learn, begin the year with readiness activities. For some children, it will be a review. For others, it will be new. For all, it will be a happy and successful start.

There is a link between readiness and handwriting/school success (Florida International University 2012). We have developed award-winning readiness materials and activities to prepare children for kindergarten and handwriting. Handwriting Without Tears® doesn't use what often passes for readiness—flat, boring pages of pencil exercises (draw a line from this to that). Instead, we've developed hands-on, multisensory activities that directly prepare children for school and handwriting.

Kindergartners need social skills for school (Boyd 2005). We model these skills with music and activities. They need to know size, shape, and position words. We teach them with the Wood Pieces Set for Capital Letters. As children rub, trade, and move the pieces, they pick up the words and concepts naturally. They need to hold and use a pencil correctly (Dennis and Swinth 2001). We help them with a song and modeling. They need beginning drawing skills (Knapton 2011). First, we build Mat Man® and then children eagerly draw people. You'll be so pleased with readiness results. We've planned guidelines for you so that your students will be ready to learn and engage through three-dimensional, musical, joyful learning that supports your teaching all year long.

Stages of Learning

Pre-Instructional Stages – Pre-K & K

Children learn to write correctly and easily when instruction follows these developmental stages. Readiness includes the many activities that develop skills. Pre-instructional readiness activities promote fine motor skills, drawing, coloring, alphabet knowledge, pre-writing, writing, number, and counting skills.

Share, Play, Socialize

Participate, take turns, and communicate with materials, music, and teacher modeling.

Make Mat Man®

Take turns. Learn body parts and how to draw with Mat Man.

Sing & Imitate

Join the class to sing about shapes, letters, numbers, and even how to say hello!

Instructional Stages – K, 1, 2

Once the pre-instructional readiness skills have been established, handwriting instruction proceeds in three stages (Imitation, Copying, and Independent Writing). It is in kindergarten where we begin formal handwriting instruction. Multisensory activities can enhance learning in every stage.

Stage 1 - Imitation

The child watches as the teacher writes and then imitates the teacher.

Stage 2 - Copying

The child looks at the completed model of a letter, word, or sentence and copies it to match the model.

Build Letters

Know how to pick and place
Wood Pieces to build letters.
(1 Big Line + 1 Big Curve = D)

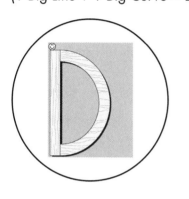

Trace on a Slate Chalkboard

Make capitals and numbers on
a reversal-proof Slate! Use the
Wet-Dry-Try activity, p. 59.

Color & Write

Practice in a child friendly
workbook with pictures and
models to promote good habits.

Stage 3 - Independent Writing

The child writes unassisted, without
a demonstration or a model.

Shake Hands with Me

Shaking hands is an important social skill. Little children can easily wave goodbye, but they now need to learn how to meet and greet people. This activity teaches this important social skill, and right and left discrimination. Each day, choose a different sensory stimulus (touch, scent, visual, auditory).

Materials
- Lotion
- Rubber stamp
- Flavor
- Cup of water

Grouping
Whole class

Support/ELL
Talk about greetings in other cultures. Be aware of the students in your room, and discuss or teach their traditions for greetings.

Activity

1. Greeting—Shake hands with each child. Smile and make eye contact.

2. Say, **Hello. This is your right hand. I'm going to do something to your right hand.**
   - Lotion—Put a dab on the right thumb. **Rub your fingers together.**
   - Rubber Stamp—Stamp the right hand. **Look at your right hand now.**
   - Flavor—Dab a flavor on the right hand to smell.
   - Water—Dip child's right fingertips in a cup. Have them shake fingers.

3. Direct students to raise their right hands and say with you, **This is my right hand. I shake hands with my right hand.**

✓Check
Observe children as they shake hands. Are they using their right hands?

More to Learn
Show children signs of left and right arrows, and talk about directions. Play a game: you hold up an arrow and children move in the direction of the arrow.

CONNECTIONS

Social Studies Link: In the United States, children can practice putting right hands over their hearts for the Pledge of Allegiance.

Getting Ready with Music

Readiness songs can bring key skills to life. Some children will already know the concepts and words, but they'll still be learning because the songs are new and exciting. Every child will benefit from practicing the skills to pay attention and respond, all while being active and engaged. Try playing the songs in the background during free play to build familiarity.

Materials
- *Rock, Rap, Tap & Learn* CD, tracks 1, 4, 6, and 9
- Wood Pieces Set for Capital Letters
- Pencils for Little Hands

Grouping
Whole class

Support/ELL
Preview position words with Big Lines. Say the words and move slowly for children to imitate.

Activity

Track 1: Alphabet Boogie
Learn alphabet knowledge with a boogie beat.

Track 4: Hey, Hey! Big Line
Positions (front, back, up, down, etc.) are fun with movement and song.

Track 6: Big Line March
This fun group song builds attention and responsiveness.
Children follow along and learn high/low, up/down, loud/soft, etc.

Track 9: Picking Up My Pencil
Use this song to learn how to pick up and hold pencils correctly.

✓ Check
Observe children as you sing. Are children joining in and learning the words?

More to Learn
Try "Hey, Hey! Big Line" without the CD. Make up your own words: "Big Line under the table, Big Line in the box, Big Line on the table."

CONNECTIONS

Language Arts Link: Songs like, "Hey, Hey! Big Line" and "Big Line March" teach about opposites. Think of other opposites with your students.

Build & Sing Mat Man®

Young children are often asked to draw pictures of themselves or of other people. Mat Man teaches drawing with building and singing. First, you build Mat Man on the floor piece by piece, and then give him away, piece by piece. Mat Man is gone, but he comes back to life with the "Mat Man" song. Children sing about each part, stopping to put it in place. They learn about body parts, where they go, and what they do. When children know how to build Mat Man, they can easily approach drawing the same way. Look at this little girl's drawing of Mat Man. See how she went from building Mat Man to drawing other people and personalizing them.

| Build | Draw | Personalize |

Mat Man

Tune: "The Bear Went Over the Mountain"

Mat Man has	**1** head,	**1** head,	**1** head	Mat Man has	**1** head	So that he can*	think
Mat Man has	**2** eyes,	**2** eyes,	**2** eyes	*(repeat)*	**2** eyes	*(repeat)*	see
Mat Man has	**1** nose,	**1** nose,	**1** nose		**1** nose		smell
Mat Man has	**1** mouth,	**1** mouth,	**1** mouth		**1** mouth		eat
Mat Man has	**2** ears,	**2** ears,	**2** ears		**2** ears		hear
Mat Man has	**1** body,	**1** body,	**1** body		**1** body	To hold what is inside*	heart, lungs, stomach
Mat Man has	**2** arms,	**2** arms,	**2** arms		**2** arms	So that he can*	reach
Mat Man has	**2** hands,	**2** hands,	**2** hands		**2** hands		clap
Mat Man has	**2** legs,	**2** legs,	**2** legs		**2** legs		stand
Mat Man has	**2** feet,	**2** feet,	**2** feet		**2** feet		walk

Materials

- Mat for Wood Pieces
- Wood Pieces Set for
  Capital Letters:
  - 2 Big Curves (head)
  - 3 Little Curves (ears, mouth)
  - 4 Big Lines (arms, legs)
  - 2 Little Lines (feet)
- Mat Man Accessories
  Pattern:
  - 2 hands
  - 2 eyes (water bottle caps)
  - 1 nose (juice cap)
  - Other items as desired

Grouping

Whole class; small group

Support/ELL

Preview activity or build a
smaller part—perhaps just
Mat Man's head.

Activity

1. Children sit on the floor in a circle.

2. You build Mat Man on the floor.

3. You give Mat Man's parts to children.

4. Children build Mat Man while singing the "Mat Man" song, p. 28.

5. Extra accessories (belly button, hair, clothing, seasonal items) make
   Mat Man more interesting or change him into a different Mat person.

✓ Check

Observe if children are anticipating each part. Check how parts are
placed. Are children actively participating?

More to Learn

Discuss what is inside the body. Print Mat Man's lungs, heart, and stomach from
A Click Away.

CONNECTIONS

Language Arts Link: Discuss concepts about print.
Read a book from the Mat Man Book Set, available
at **hwtears.com**

Technology Link: Visit Mat Man World to
play the Build Mat Man online game. Go to
hwtears.com/matman

Draw Mat Man®

Here are children's same-day drawings before and after the Mat Man activity. That means that neither time nor maturity caused the improvement. Mat Man did! Drawings done weeks later show that the improvement remains. Children's drawings will consistently be more complex (number of body parts) and accurate (parts placed correctly) than before. What changes over time is the personality of the drawings.

Mat Man Before & After

Before   After   Before   After

4-Year-Old: Same Day   4-Year-Old: Same Day

Before   After

4-Year-Old: Same Day

Materials

- Blank paper (1 per child)
- Crayons
- Easel
- Markers

Grouping

Any size

Support/ELL

Consider reviewing vocabulary words as you draw Mat Man's parts. Have children point to or move their parts as you discuss and identify Mat Man's parts.

Activity

1. Children sit at tables/desks facing you. You draw a large Mat Man at the board or easel.

2. Draw each part in order. Sing/say, **Mat Man has one head. Watch me draw the head. Now it's your turn!**

3. Continue to draw eyes, nose, mouth, ears, body, arms, hands, legs, and feet.

4. Encourage children to add other details to their drawings.

✓ Check

Observe how children hold the crayon and draw. How are their grips? Are they following your demonstration and drawing Mat Man?

More to Learn

Have students add more body parts or accessories when they repeat the activity. They may change Mat Man into another person.

CONNECTIONS

⏻ **Technology Link:** Visit Mat Man World online to share your class' Mat Man drawings. Go to **hwtears.com/matman**

Wood Pieces Set

Wood Pieces Set for Capital Letters

Set includes 26 pieces:
- 8 Big Lines
- 6 Little Lines
- 6 Big Curves
- 6 Little Curves

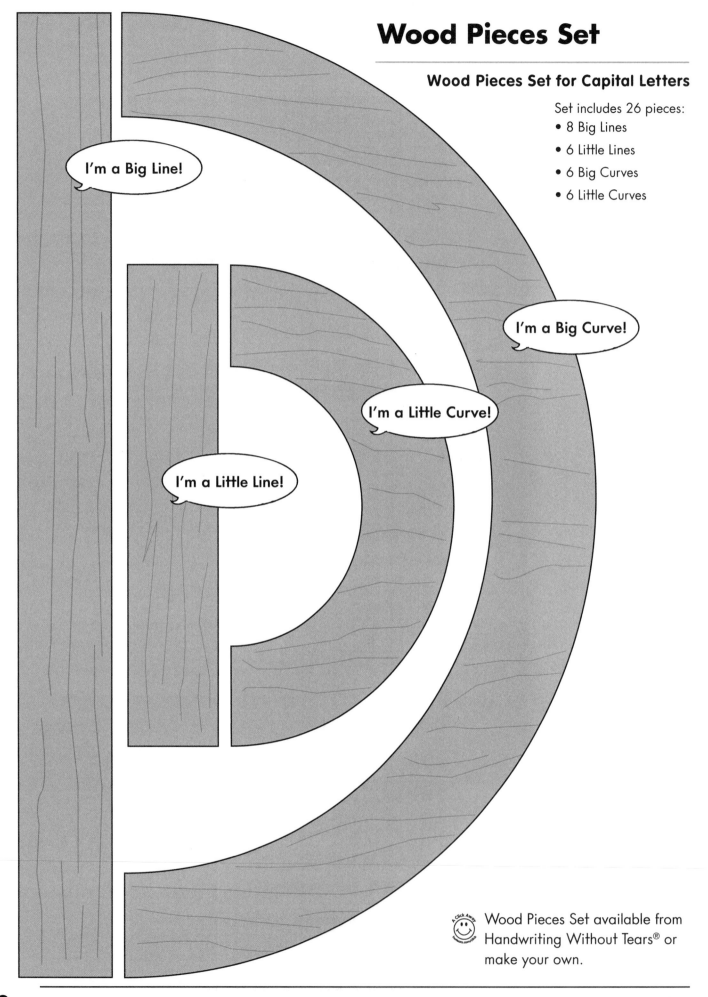

Wood Pieces Set available from Handwriting Without Tears® or make your own.

Trade, Polish & Sort Wood Pieces

Spread the Wood Pieces on the floor and have children sit around them as a group. Children love to feel like they belong. They will learn size and shape concepts, social skills, and vocabulary for building capitals—all while developing fine motor and visual skills for handwriting.

Materials
- Wood Pieces Set for Capital Letters
- Old socks or paper towels

Grouping
Whole class

Support/ELL
Make up songs as children rub the pieces to reinforce the various concepts you are teaching. Try this one to the melody of "Row, Row, Row Your Boat":

Rub, rub, rub Big Line
Rub your Big Line
Rub, rub, rub Big Line
It looks just like mine
Rub, rub, rub Big Curve
It is nice and round
Rub, rub, rub Big Curve
Now put it on the ground

Activity

1. Introduce and talk about the Wood Pieces. Gradually, they will pick up the important words (Big Line, Little Line, Big Curve, Little Curve) along with the pieces. You can say:
   You have a Big Curve. I have a Big Curve. We picked the same pieces.
   You have a Big Line. I have a Big Curve. Do you want to trade?

2. Polish the Wood Pieces. You can say:
   Let's polish lines. Do you want to polish a Big Line or a Little Line?
   It's time to collect the Wood Pieces. Who has a Big Line?

✓ Check
Observe children to see which hand they use to rub the Wood Pieces. Generally, it will be the dominant hand. Do children name the Wood Pieces correctly?

More to Learn
Collect and put away the Wood Pieces, sorting them by size and shape. Finding the right pieces among others is a figure-ground (visual) activity. Stacking requires turning and positioning.

CONNECTIONS

Math Link: Have children categorize and count the number of Wood Pieces by size or shape. Students can also create patterns with their Wood Pieces.

Positions & Body Parts with Wood Pieces

Children use position words to follow directions. It's so much fun to follow you, "Big Line **up** in the air, **under** your chair, **over** your head, **under** your arm." As children play, they learn position words and body parts. As they follow you, they learn to imitate, focus, and respond quickly.

Materials
• Wood Pieces Set for Capital Letters

Grouping
Whole class; small group

Support/ELL
Show pictures of people. Have children point to different body parts on the picture. Say the body part out loud as you point.

Activity

1. Say the name of each position as you demonstrate. Have children join in. (See illustrations.)

2. Teach other position words such as: **behind** my back, **between** my fingers, **beside** me, **through** my arm (put hand on hip first), **on** my lap, **on** my shoulder.

3. When teaching **top**, **bottom**, **middle**, use a Big Line. Hold the Big Line with just one hand at the **bottom**, then change hands and positions, naming the position each time. Children imitate.

4. Teach body parts by naming each body part as you touch it with a Wood Piece.

✓ Check
Name the positions for children to imitate. Can they move their Wood Pieces to that position?

More to Learn
Play "Teacher Says" (just like Simon Says) and move Wood Pieces in different positions.

Hold the Big Line **up** in the air.
Move it **up** and **down**.

Hold the Big Line **under** your chair.
Move it **under** your arm,
and **over** your arm.

Hold the Big Line **out** to one side.
Move it **around** in a circle.

Hold the Big Line in **front** of you.
Move it **behind** your back,
between your fingers.
Hold it at the **bottom**, it's **vertical**.

Climb **up** and **down** the Big Line.
Hold it at the **top**, **middle**,
and **bottom**.

Hold the Big Line **horizontal**.
Move it **side** to **side**.

CONNECTIONS

Language Arts Link: Use position words, also known as prepositions, to describe objects in the room. "The book is **on** the table," or "My snack is **in** my backpack."

Math Link: Using Big Lines, have children find objects that are longer, shorter, and the same size as their lines.

Curves & Circles

By imitating you, children prepare for capitals made with curves: **B, C, D, G, O, P, Q, R, S, U**. Children learn that **O** can be letter **O**, number **O**, or an **O** shape. When children rotate their arms to make circles, they prepare to write **O** and draw anything with a circular shape: snowmen, wheels, faces.

Materials
- Wood Pieces Set for Capital Letters:
  - 2 Big Curves or 2 Little Curves (per child)

Grouping
Whole class; small group

Support/ELL
The symbol **O** has three different names: circle, zero, and letter **O**. Help children understand that all three names belong. Focus on each concept individually.

Activity

1. Give each child two Big Curves or two Little Curves.

2. Say the name of each position as you demonstrate. Have children say it, too. (See illustrations.)

3. Teach **O** as a letter, a number, and a shape.

✔ Check
Observe children with the Big Curves and Little Curves. Are they able to make a circle, zero, and letter **O**?

More to Learn
Sing the song "Somewhere Over the Rainbow" to teach the rainbow shape and the concept **over**. Go on an **O** hunt around the room.

Apart
Hold the Big Curves **apart**.

Together
Bring them **together**.

O or zero
Say "**O**" or "**Zeeeero.**"
Hold up two Big Curves to your face.
Look at a friend's **O**. Make circles in
the air now.

Rainbow
Hold **up** a Big Curve.
Hold the Big Curve, and then
trace **over** the rainbow with
the other hand.

Smile
Hold up a Big Curve to make
a happy face. Turn it **down**
to make a sad face.

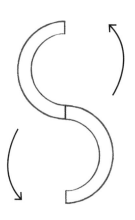

Squiggle-Wiggle
Hold up two Big Curves with
just one end touching. Move
them alternately **up** or **down**.

CONNECTIONS

Language Arts Link: Use a Big Curve as a prop, and
have children talk about what makes them smile. Model
for children "I smile when..." or "I smile because..."

Vertical, Horizontal & Diagonal Positions

By imitating you, children learn the concepts of vertical, horizontal, and diagonal. They need to know how to place lines horizontally and vertically for letters **E, F, H, I, L, T**. Diagonals prepare children for capitals **A, K, M, N, R, V, W, X, Y, Z**.

Materials
- Wood Pieces Set for Capital Letters
  - 2 Big Lines (per child)
  - 1 Little Line (per child)

Grouping
Whole class; small group

Support/ELL
Encourage children to speak with you. The words vertical, horizontal, and diagonal are fun to say with the motions. Teach concepts one at a time.

Activity
1. Give each child two Big Lines.
2. Use the position words **vertical**, **horizontal**, and **diagonal**, and have children say them as they imitate you. (See illustrations.)
3. Introduce the capitals **V, T, A, X** as they make them with you.

✓ Check
Observe their handedness as children play. Do most move their Wood Pieces with their dominant hand?

More to Learn
Show two children holding **V** how to make them touch for **W**.

Hold two Big Lines **together** in one hand.

Open them! Hold them **out**. Say, Voilà! It's a **V**. Help children finger trace **V**.

Hold two Big Lines **end** to **end** diagonally. Move and say, **diagonal**, **diagonal**.

Make a Big Line stand **up**. It's **vertical**. Make it walk **on** your arm.

Now it's tired. Make it lie **down**. It's **horizontal**.

One Big Line is standing **up**. One Little Line **across** the **top**. It's capital **T**.

Hold one Big Line **in** each hand. They are **vertical**.

Put them **together** at the **top**. Looks like a teepee or start of **A**.

Together at the **middle**— It's **X**! **X** marks the spot!

CONNECTIONS

Math Link: Have children build a structure with blocks. Encourage them to use vertical, horizontal, and diagonal positions and explain what they made.

Home Link: Send home these new vocabulary words. To download this activity, visit **hwtears.com/click**

Alphabet Knowledge

ABC blocks are classic toys because the ABC's are the building blocks for reading and writing. The ABC's are already in children's lives in Pre-K, and with the right experiences, their alphabet knowledge blossoms. In turn, this helps children get off to the right start in kindergarten. Children learn to name letters as you teach them how to build and write letters. Most children will recognize and identify the letters in their names first.

Alphabet knowledge develops in stages. It starts with singing the ABC's correctly from **A** to **Z**. Then it's a matter of putting letter names and letter symbols together (Strickland and Schickedanz 2009). Entering kindergarten, most children know a few letters by sight. Even children who don't know letters by sight can point to and say letters one by one when the letters are in ABC order. As alphabet knowledge grows, children expand their sight letter repertoire and learn to name letters in any order.

Capitals are the key to the development of letter recognition. They are the first letters children can recognize (NAEYC and IRA 1998). It helps that each capital is so distinctive. Even before children can name letters, they can recognize and find them. If you ask, "Where is **O**?" a child may point to **O** in **STOP**. But if you ask, "What is this letter?" the same child may not remember **O**. Gradually, children learn to both recognize (know what a letter looks like) and name (remember and say the name) all the capitals.

Capitals make lowercase letters easy. Children who learn capitals first can easily distinguish capitals from lowercase letters. They learn lowercase letters quickly because they already know all the lowercase letters that are the same as (**c**, **o**, **s**, **v**, **w**, **x**, **z**) or similar to (**j**, **k**, **p**, **t**, **u**, **y**) the capitals. They already know other lowercase letters from their names.

Any time children are interacting with letters, they are building alphabet knowledge. However, it's important to know that alphabet knowledge has to be explicitly taught. In our kindergarten program, we build these important skills by singing, building, pointing, tracing, and writing letters. Remember, just as receptive language comes before expressive language, children can recognize and point to a named letter before they can look at a letter and name it.

This activity is a crowd pleaser. Children enjoy the suspense (What letter will it be?) and the affirmation (I knew it would be **D**.). Keep the name of each new letter a secret until you finish writing it. Children will be excited to repeat this activity.

Materials
- Whiteboard or blackboard with wide stop line near bottom
- Erasable crayon, marker, or chalk

Grouping
Whole class

Support/ELL
Help children start at the top. Make stopping easy by using a wide stopping line at first.

Activity

1. Write **A**, describing each step: **Big Line, Big Line, Little Line.**

2. Ask, **Whose name begins with A?** Wait for children to respond. **Adam's name begins with A.**

3. Introduce Adam. Pause to let children finish your sentences.
   This is . . . Adam. Adam starts with letter . . . A.
   The first sound in Adam is . . . /a/.

4. Adam signs in with a Big Line down from **A**. He stops on the line. Continue to write letters so that children can sign in alphabetically.

✓ Check
Observe handedness. Do children slow down to stop on the line?

More to Learn
After you complete the activity, discuss the results. How many children have the same letter? Count and compare the number of lines for each letter.

CONNECTIONS

Math Link: For a morning message, have children add a line to their letter for a survey question. Do you like ice cream? Do you have a pet?

Kindergarten Teacher's Guide: Foundation Skills

Preparing for Paper & Pencil

Three Easy Steps

When it comes to handwriting, children must be taught everything! That includes how to sit, position the paper, and hold a pencil. This is the physical approach to handwriting. Sometimes it's the physical approach, not the letters and numbers, that causes a child to have trouble with handwriting. Think of it like playing a musical instrument. If you don't know how to position yourself and hold the instrument correctly, how can you play beautiful music? The same is true with writing letters and numbers. The ability to position yourself and hold your pencil correctly has a lot to do with being able to write legibly.

Important questions:
- How do you get children to sit up while writing?
- How do you position the paper?
- What is the secret to a good pencil grip?

Step 1 – Posture

Does the furniture fit? The right size and style of chair and desk affect school performance. Children don't come in a standard size! Check that every child can sit with feet flat on the floor and arms resting comfortably. Children who sit on their feet often will lose stability in their upper torso. On the following page, we show you how good posture can be fun. We have a secret for getting children to stop sitting on their feet.

Step 2 – Paper Placement

There's a misconception that people should slant their paper to make slanted writing. Not true. In fact, we slant paper so that it fits the natural arc of the forearm. Children who slant their papers properly can write faster because the arm moves naturally with the paper.

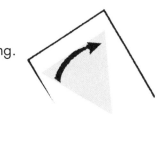

Step 3 – Grasping Grip

The most important thing to understand about pencil grip is that it doesn't develop naturally—it is learned. Based on our years of experience helping children, we developed our own theories about how to develop good pencil grip habits effectively. Because children are born imitators, demonstration will lead to success.

On the next few pages, you will find fun strategies to help you teach posture, paper, and pencil skills.

Stomp Your Feet

Stomping is fun and really works! Students' feet will be on the floor and parallel in front of them. The arm movements make their trunks straight. The noise lets them release energy, but it's under your control. When you have them stop stomping, they'll have good posture and be ready to pay attention. Use Stomp Your Feet a few times a day.

Materials
None

Grouping
Whole class

Support/ELL
While doing the motions, say the words out loud: "stomping," "pulling," "pushing."

Activity

1. Sit down and show the children how to stomp their feet and wave their arms.

2. Have them shout, "Na, na, naaaah, na, na naaah," with you as they wave and stomp.

3. Have children push and pull their hands. Have them hug themselves. (See illustrations.)

4. End by having children raise their shoulders up, pull shoulders back, and let them down.

✓ Check

Check posture. Are children sitting in a more upright position, and ready to write?

More to Learn

Use "Stomp Your Feet," track 10, from the *Rock, Rap, Tap & Learn* CD. Children push their chairs away from their desks and follow along.

Push palms

Pull hands

Hug yourself tightly

Raise shoulders

Pull shoulders back

Let them down

CONNECTIONS

▶ **Video Lesson:** View "Stomp Your Feet" at **hwtears.com/videos**

Paper Placement & Pencil Grip

Place the Paper

How do you position paper correctly? Most children naturally place a bowl of ice cream in front of them. They may, however, lean over in an awkward position to write. Children who put their paper in front of them and slant it properly can write more efficiently because they position their arms naturally with the paper. You need to teach them how to place their papers appropriately. Have your students turn to p. 6 in *Letters and Numbers for Me*, and teach them how to slant their papers for their handedness.

Children who are able to print sentences across the page are ready to tilt the paper at a slight angle to follow the natural arc of the writing hand. The correct way to tilt the paper is easy to remember (see illustrations below). For right-handed children, put the right corner higher; for left-handed children, put the left corner higher. The writing hand is below the line of writing. This practice encourages a correct, neutral wrist position.

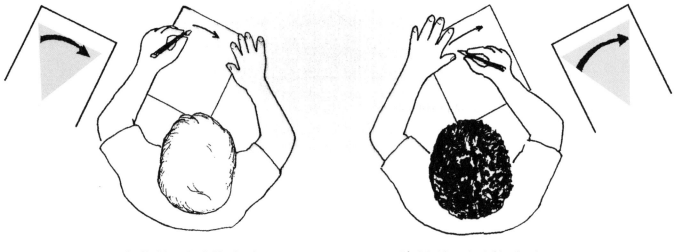

Left–Handed Students   **Right–Handed Students**

Looking Out for Lefties

You might observe some left-handed children slanting their papers too much. They do this to prevent their wrists from hooking. You can allow them to exaggerate the slant on their papers if it doesn't cause speed or neatness trouble. Visit **hwtears.com/click** for more information about the left-handed writing position.

Cross Strokes

When writing, we typically travel from top to bottom and left to right. At times, left-handed children may choose to cross letters by pulling their writing hand from right to left. This is natural. Model it for them in their workbooks for the letters below.

Mark arrows → for right-handed students. Mark arrows ← for left-handed students.

A E F f G H I J T t

Grasping Grip

Educators often have questions about pencil grip. We are frequently asked why awkward pencil grips happen and how to correct them. We seldom hear about how to prevent them. A good pencil grip does not develop naturally. In fact, several factors affect how a child learns to hold a pencil correctly. Below are 10 things we often think about regarding grip:

1. Experiences
We develop pencil grip habits while we are young. Children who are encouraged to feed themselves have more fine motor experiences than those who are spoon fed. Children who have early self-feeding experiences may have an easier time learning how to hold their crayons and pencils.

2. Toys
Today's toys are very different from those with which we grew up. We should always encourage and remind families about non-battery operated toys because they help build hand strength.

3. Imitation
Children are born imitators. When they are watching you write, always demonstrate a correct grip because they tend to do as you do.

4. Early Instruction
Help children place their fingers. Teach Pre-K children and kindergartners their finger names and finger jobs and show them how their fingers should hold writing tools.

5. Tool Size
Choose appropriate writing tools. We prefer little tools: Little Sponge Cubes, Little Chalk Bits, FLIP Crayons®, and Pencils for Little Hands. These tools promote using the finger tips naturally. Big tools elicit a fisted grip; little tools, a more mature grip. As adults, we write with pencils that are in proportion to our hands. Children should do the same.

6. Timing
It is difficult to correct the grips of older children because we have to re-teach their motor patterns. Older children need time to get used to a new way of holding a pencil. It takes repetition, persistence, and practice.

7. Blanket Rules
Avoid blanket rules about pencil grip devices. Some devices may work for a child. If they are motivating and work, use them. Use grip devices as a last resort and use them for older children who understand their purpose.

8. Acceptance
Some awkward pencil grips are functional. If the child is comfortable and doesn't have speed or legibility issues, let it go.

9. Joints
We are all made differently. Some of us have joints that are more relaxed. Therefore, expect slight variations in what is considered a standard grip. If a child is unable to use a standard grip, you may consider an altered grip as illustrated. The pencil is placed between the index and middle fingers.

10. Summer
This is the perfect time to change an awkward grip. Take advantage of the child's down time to create new habits.

The Correct Grip

The standard way for children to hold their pencil is illustrated below. If you write using a grip that is different than tripod or quadropod, alter your grip for classroom demonstration.

Tripod Grip

Standard grip: Hold pencil with
thumb + index finger.
Pencil rests on middle finger.

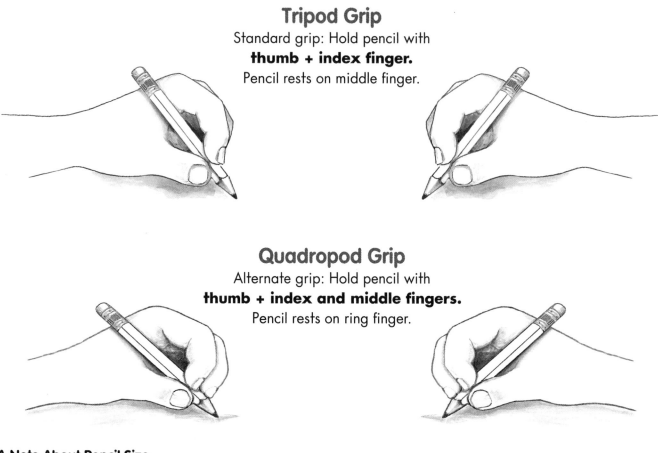

Quadropod Grip

Alternate grip: Hold pencil with
thumb + index and middle fingers.
Pencil rests on ring finger.

A Note About Pencil Size

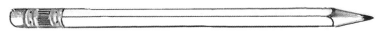

Start by using golf-size pencils in kindergarten and first grade. As children gain handwriting experience, their control will improve. Typically, as children gain more control in first grade, they will be ready for a standard-size pencil.

Flip the Pencil Trick

Here is another method. It is a trick that someone introduced to us at a workshop. It's such fun that we love to share it. Children like to do it and it puts the pencil in the correct position. (Illustrated for right-handed students.)

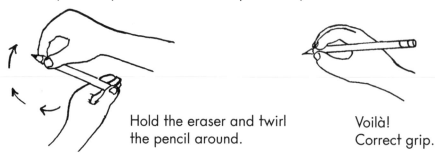

Place pencil on table pointing away from you. Pinch the pencil on the paint where the paint meets the wood.

Hold the eraser and twirl the pencil around.

Voilà! Correct grip.

Use this song from the *Rock, Rap, Tap & Learn* CD to make your pencil grip lessons more memorable. You sing the first verse, and students will join in the second.

Materials

- *Rock, Rap, Tap & Learn* CD, "Picking Up My Pencil," track 9
- Pencil Pick-Ups
- *Letters and Numbers for Me*

Grouping

Whole class

Support/ELL

If a child struggles to position the pencil, place it in their fingers correctly. Name their fingers as you position them on the pencil.

Activity

1. Listen to "Picking Up My Pencil" as background music a few times with your students.

2. For fun, review the names of the penicl grip fingers: thumb, pointer, tall man (middle finger).

3. Without the CD, sing and demonstrate the first verse.

4. In the second verse, children will sing with you. They pick up their pencils, check their own grip, and their neighbor's, too.

Note: The fast pace of the song is to encourage students to pick up the tune quickly, and to inspire them to sing it on their own.

✓ Check

Check to see if children are holding up the correct fingers as modeled and requested. Do they hold their pencil the right way?

More to Learn

Practice pencil grips on paper. Use Pencil Pick-Ups from p. *7* of *Letters and Numbers for Me* or download at **hwtears.com/click**

CONNECTIONS

▶ **Video Lesson:** View "Teaching Grip" at **hwtears.com/videos**

⌂ **Home Link:** Families can help children hold their pencils correctly, too. Send home information about pencil grip, available at **hwtears.com/click**

Emergent Writing

Fine Motor Skills

Often, kindergarten children (especially boys) need some additional fine motor support. If you think a child may have a fine motor delay, consider speaking to an occupational therapist.

Most children's upper body strength and motor coordination develop through play. Playground equipment helps children develop the strength and coordination required for fine motor skills. Some children may never have the opportunity to use playground equipment, so allow time in your day for them to experience the benefits of monkey bars, swings, and other great playground equipment.

Remember, we live in a world of technology. Toys are different today than they were several years ago. Be picky and select toys that require hand skills to move pieces, manipulate parts, or snap things together. Doing so will help children develop fine motor control.

Visit **hwtears.com/click** for Fine Motor & Letter Practice for Home download.

Learning to Write

Handwriting skills will emerge with proper instruction. When children enter kindergarten, we have no way of knowing their handwriting experience. Regardless of their level of preparedness, you can help them to become emergent writers by showing them the way. Learning handwriting is similar to learning to ride a bike. We start by giving the child a tricycle, then training wheels, and finally two wheels. Unfortunately, in today's world, too often we find ourselves giving the two wheels before the training.

Handwriting develops along a skill continuum. Between the ages of birth and two, children develop critical hand skills through self-feeding, exploring, touching, and playing. Around the age of two, children become interested in crayons and make random marks and scribbles. By age three, children begin to use lines and circular strokes that may look like letters or numbers (Gessell 1940). Coloring and drawing develop a child's ability to write (Knapton 2011). Seeing how you or a family member holds and moves the crayon to make lines, circles, pictures, and letters prepares children for writing. Teachers and families need to show children how to hold their writing tools, and how to use the helper hand (the hand that holds the paper). Between four and five years of age there is an obvious interest in forming letters through exploration. More formalized handwriting instruction should begin.

Emergent writers should learn to write their names first. Use techniques of imitation/demonstration so that children can learn to write simple words with correct letter formation. Before children are able to write on their own, you should draw upon the Language Experience Approach. Tompkins defines this approach as a teacher writing a student's dictated composition and using the text for reading instruction; it is usually used with beginning readers (2010). In the illustration, you see how the teacher wrote what the child dictated.

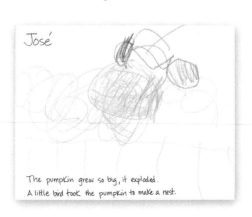

José

The pumpkin grew so big, it exploded. A little bird took the pumpkin to make a nest.

Journal Writing

Journal writing in kindergarten is a common practice. When is it appropriate for kindergartners to write in journals? The answer depends on the function of the journal and what you are hoping to teach.

To give children the best experience for success, teach them their letters first and then have them transition to journal writing as they develop the ability to combine letters into words and words into sentences. As ideal as that sounds, we also understand there are several reasons beyond handwriting for exposing children to journal writing.

Journal writing in kindergarten is similar to free writing. As long as students get proper handwriting instruction, journal writing should not be a problem. You might not have the best looking journals in the first few months of school, but if you want to expose students to the process of writing, then it's okay to introduce journal writing.

Tips

1. Have beginning writers draw a picture as an adult models the writing.

2. Choose words from a group of letters the children have learned in handwriting. For example, after they learn **c**, **o**, **s**, **v**, **w**, **a**, **d**, and **g**, you can model the words "dog," "good," "dad," etc., for them to write in their journals. They can then draw a picture of their choice.

3. Consider waiting until students have learned all of their lowercase letters. See the example below. This child drew a picture at the start of the school year.

In the fall, the child's teacher modeled the writing.   By spring, the child was writing independently.

WRITING CAPITALS

Capitals are big, bold, and important. They deserve a very important place in developing strong handwriting skills. Teachers agree and task analysis shows that capitals are easier to learn than lowercase letters (NAEYC and IRA 1998).

We teach developmentally, so we teach capitals first. We teach the capital letters as a group, separate from lowercase. Instead of teaching 52 letter symbols with a mishmash of different sizes, positions, and confusing starting places, we divide and conquer. We cut the learning task in half and begin with 26—not 52—letters.

The 26 capitals are the easiest letters to learn. They are easy to recognize because each has a personality and an individual, distinctive look (NAEYC and IRA 1998). Capitals are the easiest because of their simplicity. They are made of four shapes—Big Lines, Little Lines, Big Curves, and Little Curves. They are all the same size (tall) with the same starting place (top). They all occupy the same vertical position in space.

We introduce capitals with multisensory, hands-on letter lessons. This makes an easy transition from building to writing in the workbook. In the workbook, the focus is on writing habits. In every lesson, throughout the year, you help children with the physical habits for writing: posture, pencil grip, and using the helper hand.

In every lesson, you model letter formations for students. You show them how to start at the top and how to make every stroke in the right sequence. We've grouped the capitals to make this easy. Letters are organized by how they're made. Each lesson builds on the lesson before, and gradually good habits become automatic. Building good habits with capitals (correct formation, no reversals) is an exclusive Handwriting Without Tears® feature. We have carefully planned the curriculum to help you develop strong handwriting skills for every child, from the very first lesson.

Developmental Teaching

Handwriting Skill Progression

When children learn to write their capitals, they develop a strong foundation for printing. Children learn to:
- Start letters at the top.
- Use the correct stroke sequence to form letters.
- Orient letters and numbers correctly—no reversals!

When capitals are taught first, learning lowercase letters is a breeze. Think about it: **c**, **o**, **s**, **v**, **w** and **x**, **y**, and **z** are the same as their capitals; **j**, **k**, **t**, **p**, and **u** are also similar to their capital partners. If we teach capitals correctly, we have already prepared children for nearly half of the lowercase alphabet.

Some capitals are developmentally easier to write than others. Children gradually develop the ability to copy forms in a predictible order (Gesell 1940).

| up to 3-years-old | up to 4-years-old | up to 6-years-old |

Developmental Analysis – Capitals Vs. Lowercase Letters

This is the capital/lowercase analysis that informs our developmental teaching order.

Capital Letters Are Easy
- All start at the top.
- All are the same height.
- All occupy the same vertical space.
- All are easy to recognize and identify (compare **A**, **B**, **D**, **G**, **P**, **Q** with **a**, **b**, **d**, **g**, **p**, **q**).
- All are big, bold, and familiar.

Lowercase Letters Are More Difficult
- Lowercase letters start in four different places (**a**, **b**, **e**, **f**).
- Lowercase letters are not all the same size:
  - -14 letters are half the size of capitals.
  - -12 are the same size as capitals.
- Lowercase letters occupy three different vertical positions: small, tall, descending.
- Lowercase letters are more difficult to recognize because of subtle differences (**a**, **b**, **d**, **g**, **p**, **q**).

Let's Do the Math

You can see at a glance that capitals are easier for children. Students have fewer chances to make mistakes when they write capital letters. They aim their pencil at the top and get it right. With lowercase, there are many more variables.

CAPITAL & LOWERCASE LETTER ANALYSIS		
	Capitals	Lowercase
Start	1	4
Size	1	2
Position	1	3
Appearance	• Familiar • Distinctive A, B, D, G, P, Q	• Many similar • Easy to confuse a, b, d, g, p, q

Hands-On Letter Activities

Hands-On Letter Actvities are a child friendly way to teach children to write. Children can learn writing skills before they even put pencil to paper. They can learn how to make letters right side up and facing correctly. These lessons provide the fun of multisensory play while enabling you to teach correct handwriting habits from the start.

Capital Letter Cards for Wood Pieces

Each card shows a different letter made with Wood Pieces. Children use real Wood Pieces to cover the letter in the correct order, piece by piece. These cards are ideal for teaching the first letters in children's names. Each child has his/her own letter. You help each child choose the correct Wood Pieces and place them in order. Always use the correct Wood Piece words. For example, **R** is made with a Big Line, then a Little Curve, then a Little Line.

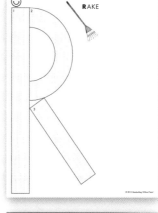

Capitals on the Mat for Wood Pieces

The Mat is a place to build Wood Piece letters. It has a smiley face in the top left corner. That is the cue children need to place the Wood Pieces and make letters correctly. You build each letter correctly, step by step, and children imitate.

Sometimes you may keep the name of the letter you are building a secret. Children like a surprise. This is an easy way for children to learn letter names and good habits for making letters.

Wet-Dry-Try on the Slate Chalkboard

What's this? It's Wet-Dry-Try. This multisensory activity engages all learning styles. It's visual, auditory, kinesthetic, and tactile. You write a chalk letter. Then, children wet, dry, and try the letter with chalk. The latest research on brain development supports this activity. Brain research calls for fewer elements, teacher modeling, sensory engagement, and immediate feedback (Sousa 2011).

Teacher's Part   **Child's Part**

  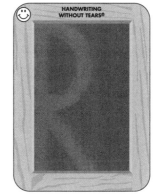 

Model   Wet   Dry   Try

Top to Bottom

English is a top-to-bottom, left-to-right language. Teaching a top-to-bottom habit is the secret to handwriting success. Children who start letters at the top develop speed and neatness. Those who start from the bottom generally struggle with handwriting.

Often, we judge a young child's writing only by how the letters look. Do not be misled by the appearance of children's letters and numbers. Children's fluency, and ultimately, their neatness depends on their habits for letter and number formation. This is particularly true when writing demands increase. Try this experiment:

Make five lines down, slowly.   **Make five lines, alternating down/up.**   **Now do it again, quickly.**

↓ **slowly** | | | (| ↓↑ **slowly** | | (| | ↓ **quickly** (| | (| ↓↑ **quickly** (| \ | |

Notice that when you make lines slowly, it doesn't really matter where you start. But, when you add speed, it does matter where you start. Children who start at the top can be fast and neat! Tell families about this. Send children home singing this song to remind families to help children start at the top.

Where Do You Start Your Letters?
Tune: "If You're Happy and You Know It"

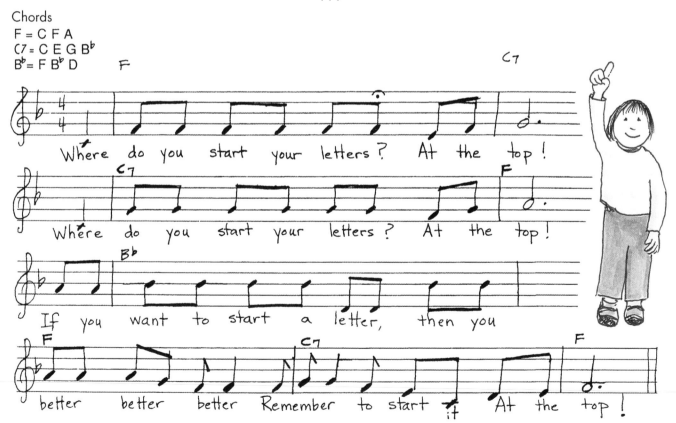

Where Do You Start Your Letters?

Children never forget where to start their letters with this fun song. Not only are they moving and having fun, they are learning prepositions, too!

Materials
- *Rock, Rap, Tap & Learn* CD, "Where Do You Start Your Letters?" track 2

Grouping
Whole class

Support/ELL
Teach the meaning of the word "top" with Wood Pieces. Have children hold the "top" of a Big Line. See Foundation Skills section, p. 35.

Activity

1. Play "Where Do You Start Your Letters?" in the background as children play so they will become familiar with the lyrics. They'll know the tune from "If You're Happy and You Know It."

2. Sing the song with children. Make a questioning gesture with hands for "Where?" and point high for "At the top!"

3. End by writing a letter on the board.

✓ Check
Observe as children build a letter with the Wood Pieces. Can they identify the top/correct starting point?

More to Learn
Make a lyric change with "Where Do You Start Your Numbers?"

CONNECTIONS

🏠 **Home Link:** Explain to families the importance of starting letters at the top! Send home information and lyrics to the song, available at **hwtears.com/click**

Capital Letter Cards for Wood Pieces

Capital Letter Cards show a capital made with Wood Pieces. Children put real Wood Pieces on the card. This is a great first letter play activity, especially for children who are just learning to turn and place pieces. Children build the letters piece by piece. It's also a beginning activity for observation and organization.

Materials
- Capital Letter Cards for Wood Pieces
- Wood Pieces Set for Capital Letters

Grouping
Small group

Support/ELL
Placing each piece requires fine motor control and spatial awareness. Help to place a piece, take it away, and then let a child try.

Activity

1. Place a different Capital Letter Card in front of each child. Have them point to the ☺. This shows that the letter is right side up.
2. Point to each child's Letter Card. Say, **This is capital _____. What pieces do you need for _____? That's right. Collect the pieces. Put them near your card. Then wait until everyone is ready.**
3. Place the pieces as a group, like this:
   Pick up the first piece for your letter. Wait for everybody. Put it in place.
   Pick up the second piece. Wait... everyone ready? Put it in place.
   Pick up the third piece. Wait... everyone ready? Put it in place. You made _____.

✓ Check
Observe if children choose the right pieces. Do they place and name the Wood Pieces correctly?

More to Learn
Instead of building random letters, give children the card for the first letter in their names.

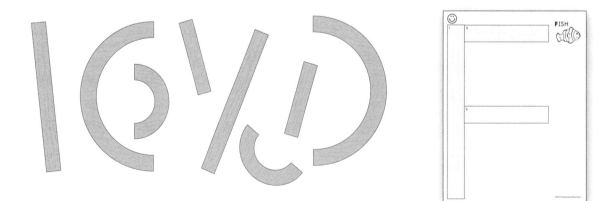

CONNECTIONS

▶ **Video Lesson:** View "Building Capitals with Capital Letter Cards" at **hwtears.com/videos**

Capitals on the Mat for Wood Pieces

The Mat for Wood Pieces is blue with a yellow smiley face in the top left corner. That's the Starting Corner for **B, D, E, F, H, K, L, M, N, P, R, U, V, W, X, Y,** and **Z.** Many of them (**B, D, E, F, H, K, L, M, N, P, R**) start with a Big Line on the left side. When the Big Line is on the left, the next part of the letter is always on the right side of the Big Line.

Materials
- Wood Pieces Set for Capital Letters
- Mat for Wood Pieces
- Wood Pieces Letter Chart

Grouping
Whole class; small group

Support/ELL
Start with simple two- or three-piece letters. Explicitly teach the words: big, little, top, middle, bottom. Have children repeat the words.

Activity

1. Scatter the Wood Pieces on the floor in front of children.

2. Give each child a Mat to place right side up. The smiley face will be at the top left. Make sure your Mat is in the same orientation as theirs.

3. Build a letter piece by piece for children to imitate. To see the sequence for any letter, refer to the Wood Pieces Letter Chart.

4. Describe each step as you build the letter:
   I put the Big Line here, under the ☺. Your turn.
   I put a Little Line at the top. Your turn.
   I put another Little Line at the middle. It's letter _____!

✓ Check
Observe as students build letters. Do they know the letter when it's finished?

More to Learn
Teach all the letters except **U** and **J** on the Mat. Letters **A, C, G, I, O, Q, S,** and **T** are Center Starting Capitals. They start at the top center of the Mat.

Demonstrate

CONNECTIONS

▶ **Video Lesson:** View "Building Capitals Letters on the Mat" at **hwtears.com/videos**

🏠 **Home Link:** Teach families how to teach capitals, too. Send home Capital Letter Charts, available at **hwtears.com/click**

Show Me Magnetic Pieces for Capitals™

This activity teaches correct letter formation as you demonstrate for the entire class using a vertical surface. Children can all see you as they build letters with their own Wood Pieces and Mat.

Materials
- Show Me Magnetic Pieces for Capitals
- Wood Pieces Set for Capital Letters
- Mat for Wood Pieces

Grouping
Whole class

Support/ELL
Say the names of the Magnetic Pieces while holding them up. Have children imitate you with their Wood Pieces.

Activity

1. Scatter the Wood Pieces on the floor in front of children.

2. Give each child a Mat to place right side up. The smiley face will be at the top.

3. Use the Show Me Magnetic Pieces to build a letter, piece by piece for children to imitate. To see the order for any letter, refer to the letter page in this teacher's guide.

4. Describe each step as you build the letter:
   I put the Big Line here, under the ☺. Your turn.
   I put a Little Curve at the top. Your turn. It's letter _____!

✓ Check
Observe if children pick up the correct Wood Piece as it is named. Do they complete the correct steps to build a letter?

More to Learn
Allow children to take turns building the first letter in their names. You demonstrate and children imitate.

CONNECTIONS

Language Arts Link: Have children say the sound associated with the letter on the magnetic board.

Wet-Dry-Try for Capitals

This is a favorite activity. You write a chalk letter and teach each step. Children wet the letter, dry it, and then try it with chalk. The Little Sponge Cubes and Little Chalk Bits reinforce correct grip. Repetition reinforces correct letter formation. Place Little Chalk Bits and Little Sponge Cubes in small cups so children can reach them.

Materials
- Slate Chalkboard (1 per child)
- Little Chalk Bits (1")
- Little Sponge Cubes (1/2")
- Little cups of water
- Paper towel pieces
- Capital Formation Chart

Grouping
Whole class; small group

Support/ELL
You say the words for each step slowly. Children join in when they can. To teach the word "wet," dip fingers in water. To emphasis "dry," dry fingers with towel. Use the Slate Chalkboard "dry" for review. Simply write and erase with a paper towel and write again.

Activity

1. Teacher's Part – Write F with Chalk
Use chalk to write a letter on double lines. Say the step-by-step directions (see below).

2. Child's Part – Wet-Dry-Try
As the child does each part, say the step-by-step directions to guide the child. The child is encouraged to join in by saying the words.
Wet: The child uses a Little Sponge Cube to trace the letter.
Dry: The child uses a little piece of paper towel to trace the letter.
Try: The child uses a Little Chalk Bit to write the letter.

✓ Check
Observe if children follow the directions. Do they complete the steps to make a letter?

More to Learn
Say the letter name and letter sound. Look for things around the room that begin with the letter.

Teacher's Part

Start in the Starting Corner,
Big Line down, Frog Jump to ☺,
Little Line across the top,
Little Line across the middle

Child's Part

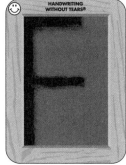

WET:
Wet **F** with sponge,
Wet **F** with wet finger,
Say the words

DRY:
Dry **F** with towel,
Dry **F** with gentle blow,
Say the words

TRY:
Try **F** with chalk,
Say the words

CONNECTIONS

▶ **Video Lesson:** View "Wet-Dry-Try" at hwtears.com/videos

Mystery Letters on the Slate Chalkboard

You can play Mystery Letters with children as a fun way to develop good habits. Mystery Letter activities teach correct letter formation. The secret is to make the first stroke correctly before telling children the name of the letter they're going to make. This ensures that students start the letter correctly.

Materials
- Slate Chalkboard (1 per child)
- Little Chalk Bits (1")
- Little Sponge Cubes (1/2")
- Little cups of water
- Paper towel pieces
- Gray Block Paper

Grouping
Whole class

Support/ELL
For children who need additional practice, consider using the Slate Chalkboard activity or having them write capitals in Gray Blocks.

Activity

1. Gather the Slate Chalkboards, Little Chalk Bits, and paper towels for erasing.

2. Say the directions as indicated below.

Note: Play the Mystery Letter games to reinforce correct habits for Starting Corner and Center Starting Capitals. You can play these games on Gray Block Paper.

✓ Check
Observe as children follow your directions. Do they start the letter correctly? Do they form it the right way?

More to Learn
Allow children to be the teacher. They can say the directions as you model the letter for the class.

For **F, E, D, P, B, R, N, M,**
Start in the Starting Corner,
Big Line down,
Frog Jump to the Starting Corner,
Now make ____

For **H, K, L,**
Start in the Starting Corner,
Big Line down,
Now make ____

For **U, V, W, X, Y, Z**
Start in the Starting Corner,
Now make ____

For **C, O, Q, G**
Start at the top center,
Make a Magic C,
Now make ____

For **S, A, I, T, J,**
Start at the top center,
Now make ____

CONNECTIONS

🔘 **Technology Link:** Use the Digital Teaching Tools to demonstrate letters for children to write. Visit **hwtears.com/dtt**

Air Writing

Air Writing is a kinesthetic strategy with visual and auditory components. Picking up and holding pencils adds a tactile component. This strategy allows you to watch the entire class and ensures that all students form their letters correctly.

Materials
- *Rock, Rap, Tap & Learn* CD, "Air Writing," track 3
- Brightly colored ball

Grouping
Whole class

Support/ELL
Show a visual of the letter you are tracing in the air. Have children trace over the visual before Air Writing.

Activity

1. Sing "Air Writing" to prepare the class for participation.

2. Choose a capital letter. Use a brightly colored ball to trace the capital letter in the air in front of your class.

3. Have students hold a pencil correctly in the air. Everyone checks pencil grips.

4. Retrace the letter again with your students.

Note: If you are facing your students, make the letter backwards in relation to you so that the letter will be correct from your students' perspective.

✓ Check
Check to see if children imitate your movements. Do they hold their pencils correctly?

More to Learn
Trace shapes in the air to review the formation and names of shapes. Try the activity with numbers.

CONNECTIONS

⏻ **Technology Link:** Use the Digital Teaching Tools to demonstrate letters for children to Air Write. Visit **hwtears.com/dtt**

Laser Letters

Children are always amazed by this activity. You can easily catch their attention when you use a small laser. By using a laser, you provide a nice visual to follow while tracing letters in the air.

Materials
- Small laser pointer*
- Chalk or markers
- Large board or easel

*In place of a laser pointer, you may also use a flashlight or other small pointer.

Grouping
Whole class

Support/ELL
To reinforce tricky letters, use the laser to trace over a visual model. Then, have children take turns finger tracing the letter.

Activity
1. Write a large letter on a board or easel, giving step-by-step directions.
2. Have students hold a pencil correctly in the air. Everyone checks pencil grips.
3. Move to the back of the room and point the laser to the start of the letter.
4. Have students point their pencils to the laser dot.
5. Use the laser to trace the letter slowly, giving step-by-step directions.
6. Have students follow with their pencils, and say the directions along with you.

✓ Check
Observe as children follow the laser. Do they form the letter correctly in the air?

More to Learn
Trace shapes in the air to review the formation and names of shapes. Try the activity with numbers.

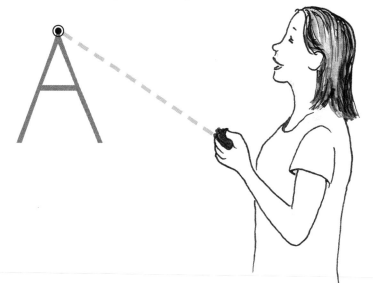

CONNECTIONS

⏻ **Technology Link:** Use the Digital Teaching Tools to demonstrate letters for children. Then, trace over letters with a laser. Visit **hwtears.com/dtt**

My Teacher Writes

Time to stretch those vocal chords! In this activity, children will love to sing in anticipation of what letter you will write. Once they guess the letter, they can all trace it together.

Materials
- *Rock, Rap, Tap & Learn* CD, "My Teacher Writes," track 21
- Large board or easel
- Markers

Grouping
Whole class

Support/ELL
Invite children to come up and trace over the letter with a different colored marker. Say the steps out loud as the child traces.

Activity

1. Children sing "My Teacher Writes" as you stand in front of the class. Change the lyrics to:

   My teacher writes a letter for me.
   What's this letter? Let's look and see.

2. Review a letter and write it in the air or on the board.

3. Have students hold a pencil correctly in the air. Everyone checks pencil grips.

4. Retrace the letters again with your students.

✓ Check

Observe as children air trace their letters. Do they trace the letters correctly? Do they use correct pencil grips?

More to Learn

Change the lyrics again by singing, "My teacher draws a shape for me. What's this shape? Let's look and see." Draw shapes on the board for review.

CONNECTIONS

⏻ **Technology Link:** Use the Digital Teaching Tools to demonstrate letters before singing the song. Visit **hwtears.com/dtt**

Capitals on the Door

Doors can do more than open and close. They can also help you teach lessons. Just put a smiley face in the top left corner, and the door is ready to help! The smiley face brings a child's eye to the top and to the Starting Corner.

Materials
- Bright yellow smiley face mounted on top left corner of door
- Small laser pointer*

*In place of a laser pointer, you may also use a flashlight or other small pointer.

Grouping
Whole class

Support/ELL
Use "wait time" before asking children to name the letter. Make children wait until you have traced the letter three times before they guess.

Activity

1. Write a laser letter on the door for all to see. What letter will it be? Write a familiar Starting Corner letter, perhaps **B, D, E, F, H, K, L, P, R, V, X,** or **Z** (hide laser beam when jumping to start another stroke).

2. Have children hold their pencils correctly in the air. Everyone checks pencil grips.

3. Children pretend to write on the door by following the laser beam.

4. Children name the letter after you finish writing.

Note: This activity also works well with numbers.

✓ Check
Observe as children trace in the air. Do they follow your laser beam with their pencils?

More to Learn
Play Guess My Letter! Children guess the letter as you trace it on the door.

CONNECTIONS

▶ **Video Lesson:** View "Capitals on the Door" at hwtears.com/videos

© 2013 Handwriting Without Tears®

Capitals with Music

Music makes learning memorable and joyful. Start by playing the CD in the background during free play. This builds familiarity. Then, when you sing during activities, children happily remember and are ready to participate.

Materials
• *Rock, Rap, Tap & Learn* CD, tracks 12, 13, 14, and 15

Grouping
Whole class

Support/ELL
Pause the CD and review portions of the song. For instance, in "Frog Jump Letters," pause and demonstrate jumping, when you sing "jumpity jump, jumpity jump."

Activity
Choose a song and an activity to go with it.

Track 12: Frog Jump Letters
Children stand up and finger trace the Frog Jump Capitals (p. 61) in the air. Let children jump around between the letter exercises.

Track 13: Give It A Middle
This song helps children learn the middle position in letter formation as they finger trace or watch as you model letters on the board.

Track 14: Give It A Top
Children learn about letters that have a top and can follow you as you model these letters on the board or in the air.

✓ Check
Observe children's gross motor skills. Do they trace letters correctly in the air?

More to Learn
Diagonals can be difficult. Teach letters **V**, **W**, **X**, **Y**, **Z** with "Sliding Down to the End of the Alphabet," track 15 from the *Rock, Rap, Tap & Learn* CD.

CONNECTIONS

▶ **Video Lesson:** View "Teaching with Music" at hwtears.com/videos

Teaching with Technology

Introducing simple technology into your daily classroom experiences can make learning letters engaging and fun. This process also exposes young children to the world of technology at an early age.

Materials
- Computer or interactive whiteboard (IWB)
- Digital Teaching Tools (available online at **hwtears.com/dtt**)

Grouping
Whole class

Support/ELL
Making large movements can help children remember letter names. For children who do not know the letters in their names, use the Digital Teaching Tools to introduce letters. Children can Air Write the letters in their names using a visual model (p. 61).

Activity

1. Choose a letter. Prepare Digital Teaching Tools (DTT) for the letter to demonstrate.

2. Children point their pointer fingers at the screen.

3. As children trace the letter, say the parts of letter.
   We are going to trace F in their air.
   Say the parts of F with me, Big Line, Little Line, Little Line.
   We made an F.

✓ Check
Observe as children trace letters in the air following the model on the screen. Do children say the correct parts of the letters as they trace?

More to Learn
Use the Digital Teaching Tools to teach lowercase letters and numbers, too.

CONNECTIONS

🔘 **Technology Link:** Use this lesson as an opportunity to discuss computers. Call children forward to activate the DTT. They will enjoy watching the letter come to life.

© 2013 Handwriting Without Tears®

Capital Teaching Order/Learn & Check

Developmental Teaching Order

The Handwriting Without Tears® teaching order is planned to help children learn handwriting skills in the easiest, most efficient way. It's also developmentally planned to start with a review of the easy letters: the capitals. They are the first letters children should learn. Your kindergartners may know them, but you want to be sure they print them correctly. The capital teaching order will help you teach:

1. Correct formation: All capitals start at the top. Strokes are made in the correct sequence.
2. Correct orientation: No reversals.

To do this, start by teaching letters in groups on Gray Blocks:

Frog Jump Capitals

These letters start at the top left corner with a Big Line on the left. When the first line is on the left, the next part of the letter is on the right side. This prevents reversals and teaches good stroke habits.

Starting Corner Capitals

Reviewing these letters ensures that children start at the top left and use the left-to-right formation habit. The good habits children form with **U, V, W, X, Y, Z** will carry over to **u, v, w, x, y, z**.

Center Starting Capitals

C O Q G S A I T J

C, O, Q, G start with a Magic C stroke. The good habits children learn here with **C, O, S, T, J** will make learning **c, o, s, t, j** much easier. There will be no problems with stroke direction or reversals.

Learn & Check

Children need to know exactly what to do.

1. Start correctly.
2. Do each step in sequence.
3. Bump the line.

Set children up for success by pointing out in their workbooks:

1. Start correctly.   **2.** Do each step.   **3.** Bump the line.

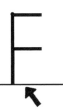

When you check their workbook letters, explain what they did right and help them correct any mistakes. After you have done this a few times, they'll begin to self-check with confidence.

Frog Jump Capitals

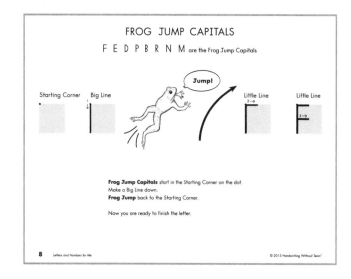

OBJECTIVE: To learn the steps for writing Frog Jump Capitals: **F, E, D, P, B, R, N,** and **M.**

Lesson Plan
Let's find the Frog Jump Capital page. Help children turn to p. 8.

1. **Demonstrate Frog Jump Capital F.**
   Demonstrate how Frog Jump Capitals start in the Starting Corner on the dot. Have children point to the first Gray Block. The Gray Block is like a picture of the Slate Chalkboard.

2. **Finger trace capital F.**
   Big Line down. Look at the next Gray Block. There is a Big Line. The Big Line goes down. Frog Jump! The frog jumps back up to the Starting Corner. It's time to finish the letter. Little Line across the top. Little Line across the middle. The letter is finished. It's capital F.

3. **Check & Evaluate**
   Evaluate children as they follow along and finger trace capital **F.**

Color
Encourage children to color the frog.

More to Learn
Use "Frog Jump Letters," track 12, *Rock, Rap, Tap & Learn* CD. While standing, finger trace Frog Jump Capitals in the air. Let children jump between singing the verses.

Support/ELL
Encourage children to say the steps out loud. Children say "Ribbit" for the Frog Jump. Making a Big Line on the left edge of the Gray Block (or Slate Chalkboard) prevents a reversal.

CONNECTIONS

▶ **Video Lesson:** View "Teaching Frog Jump Capitals" at **hwtears.com/videos**

⏻ **Technology Link:** To teach capital **F** with large movements, visit our Digital Teaching Tools at **hwtears.com/dtt**

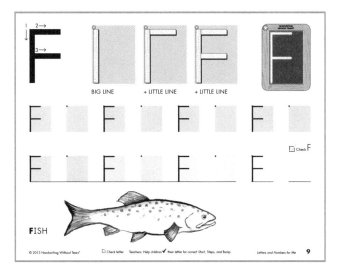

OBJECTIVE: To write capital **F** with correct formation.

Lesson Plan
Let's find the capital F page. Help children turn to p. 9. Discuss what's on the page.

1. **Demonstrate**
   Demonstrate **F** on the Slate Chalkboard, whiteboard, or flip chart.
   Use the Show Me Magnetic Pieces for Capitals™ for **F** (multisensory activity p. 58).
   Children finger trace the large capital **F** model in their workbooks.

2. **Copy**
   Prepare for writing with good posture, pencil grip, and use of the helper hand (pp. 42–44).
   Demonstrate **F** again, saying the step-by-step directions together.
   Children watch, then copy **F**'s.

3. **Check & Evaluate**
   Help children ☑ their letter for correct Start, Steps, and Bump.
   Evaluate the correct formation for capital **F**.

Read, Color & Draw
Read the word FISH together. Point out the beginning of capital **F**.
Encourage free coloring and drawing. Add water, other fish, etc.

More to Learn
This is the first page of the workbook where you ☑ the letter. Review Start, Steps, and Bump with children (p. 67).

Support/ELL
Help children make Frog Jumps after the Big Line. Model a Big Line on the board. Children should say "Ribbit" when it's time for you to jump to the top. Complete the letter. Repeat.

CONNECTIONS

Science Link: Compare and contrast frogs and fish. Discuss the meanings of amphibians and fish. Have children name other amphibians and fish.

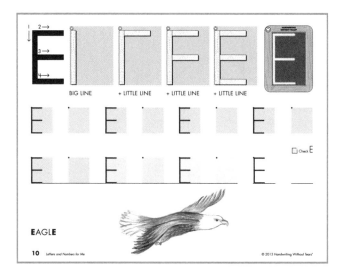

OBJECTIVE: To write capital **E** with correct formation.

Lesson Plan
Let's find the capital E page. Help children turn to p. 10. Discuss what's on the page.

1. Demonstrate
Demonstrate **E** on the Slate Chalkboard, whiteboard, or flip chart.
Use the Show Me Magnetic Pieces for Capitals™ for **E** (multisensory activity p. 58).
Children finger trace the large capital **E** model in their workbooks.

2. Copy
Prepare for writing with good posture, pencil grip, and use of the helper hand.
Demonstrate **E** again, saying the step-by-step directions together.
Children watch, then copy **E**'s.

3. Check & Evaluate
Help children ☑ their letter for correct Start, Steps, and Bump.
Evaluate the correct formation for capital **E**.

Read, Color & Draw
Read the word EAGLE together. Point out the beginning of capital **E** and the ending of **E**.
Encourage free coloring and drawing. Add clouds, other birds, etc.

More to Learn
Bring in a picture book about eagles. See if children can identify things related to eagles or other birds (e.g. trees, sky, nests, eggs).

Support/ELL
Allow left-handed children to write cross strokes from right to left. Practice top, middle, and bottom positions with a Wood Piece (pp. 34–35).

CONNECTIONS

Math Link: Bring in quarters and look at the backs of them. What do they see? Some have an eagle. Discuss the value of a quarter. Count to 25.

D

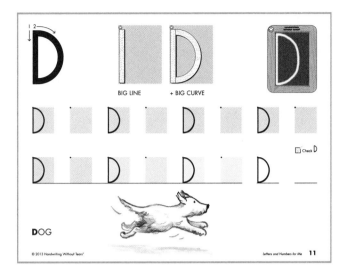

OBJECTIVE: To write capital **D** with correct formation.

Lesson Plan

Let's find the capital D page. Help children turn to p. 11. Discuss what's on the page.

1. Demonstrate

Demonstrate **D** on the Slate Chalkboard, whiteboard, or flip chart.
Use the Show Me Magnetic Pieces for Capitals™ for **D** (multisensory activity p. 58).
Children finger trace the large capital **D** model in their workbooks.

2. Copy

Prepare for writing with good posture, pencil grip, and use of the helper hand.
Demonstrate **D** again, saying the step-by-step directions together.
Children watch, then copy **D**'s.

3. Check & Evaluate

Help children ☑ their letter for correct Start, Steps, and Bump.
Evaluate the correct formation for capital **D**.

Read, Color & Draw

Read the word DOG together. Point out the beginning of capital **D**.
Encourage free coloring and drawing. Add a dog bone, dog house, etc.

More to Learn

Find the letter **D** on an ABC poster or on display cards
in your classroom. Help children name the letters before
and after **D**.

Support/ELL

If children are not ready to write letters, demonstrate letters
in Gray Blocks with a highlighter. Allow children to trace
with pencil. Practice **D** on the Slate Chalkboard (p. 59).

CONNECTIONS

Language Arts Link: Make a class list of words that
rhyme with dog.

P

OBJECTIVE: To write capital **P** with correct formation.

Lesson Plan
Let's find the capital P page. Help children turn to p. 12. Discuss what's on the page.

1. Demonstrate
Demonstrate **P** on the Slate Chalkboard, whiteboard, or flip chart.
Use the Show Me Magnetic Pieces for Capitals™ for **P** (multisensory activity p. 58).
Children finger trace the large capital **P** model in their workbooks.

2. Copy
Prepare for writing with good posture, pencil grip, and use of the helper hand.
Demonstrate **P** again, saying the step-by-step directions together.
Children watch, then copy **P**'s.

3. Check & Evaluate
Help children ☑ their letter for correct Start, Steps, and Bump.
Evaluate the correct formation for capital **P**.

Read, Color & Draw
Read the word PIG together. Point out the beginning of capital **P**.
Encourage free coloring and drawing. Add dirt, water, etc.

More to Learn
Show children capital **P** and lowercase **p**. Show them capital
F and lowercase **f**. Discuss how some letter partners look the
same and some do not. Provide another example of both.

Support/ELL
Avoid confusion with **D** and **P**. Help children make the **P**
with a Little Curve that aims for the middle. Have students
repeat the words "middle" and "bottom."

CONNECTIONS

▶ **Video Lesson:** View "Teaching Frog Jump Capitals"
at **hwtears.com/videos**

Language Arts Link: Explain that the letter **P** makes a
/**p**/ sound. What other words have a /**p**/ sound? Write
alliterative sentences together as a class.

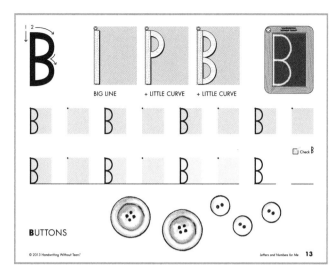

OBJECTIVE: To write capital **B** with correct formation.

Lesson Plan
Let's find the capital B page. Help children turn to p. 13. Discuss what's on the page.

1. Demonstrate
Demonstrate **B** on the Slate Chalkboard, whiteboard, or flip chart.
Use Capitals on the Door for **B** (multisensory activity p. 64).
Children finger trace the large capital **B** model in their workbooks.

2. Copy
Prepare for writing with good posture, pencil grip, and use of the helper hand.
Demonstrate **B** again, saying the step-by-step directions together.
Children watch, then copy **B**'s.

3. Check & Evaluate
Help children ☑ their letter for correct Start, Steps, and Bump.
Evaluate the correct formation for capital **B.**

Read, Color & Draw
Read the word BUTTONS together. Point out the beginning of capital **B.**
Encourage free coloring and drawing. Add more buttons.

More to Learn
Discuss buttons. Look at buttons on shirts and coats.
Discuss similarities and differences of buttons. Count button holes.

Support/ELL
For children who start at the bottom or make reversals, use the Mystery Letters on the Slate Chalkboard activity (p. 60).

CONNECTIONS

Math Link: Have children sort buttons by size, shape, color, and type. Children count total buttons by group and do simple addition.

R

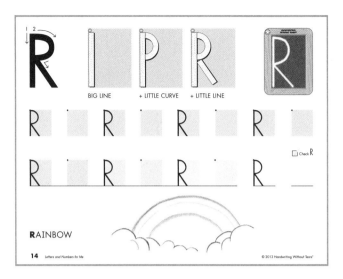

OBJECTIVE: To write capital **R** with correct formation.

Lesson Plan
Let's find the capital R page. Help children turn to p. 14. Discuss what's on the page.

1. Demonstrate
Demonstrate **R** on the Slate Chalkboard, whiteboard, or flip chart.
Use Capitals on the Door for **R** (multisensory activity p. 64).
Children finger trace the large capital **R** model in their workbooks.

2. Copy
Prepare for writing with good posture, pencil grip, and use of helper hand.
Demonstrate **R** again, saying the step-by-step directions together.
Children watch, then copy **R**'s.

3. Check & Evaluate
Help children ☑ their letter for correct Start, Steps, and Bump.
Evaluate the correct formation for capital **R**.

Read, Color & Draw
Read the word RAINBOW together. Point out the beginning of capital **R**.
Encourage free coloring and drawing. Add raindrops, sun, etc.

More to Learn
Use "Diagonals," track 5, *Rock, Rap, Tap & Learn* CD.
While standing, make the diagonal motion in the air.
Show children what diagonal looks like in the letter **R**.

Support/ELL
This style of **R** uses only two strokes. Encourage students to
make the Little Curve and Little Line in one continuous stroke.

CONNECTIONS

Science Link: Discuss rainbows. What are the colors
in a rainbow? What causes a rainbow? Look at pictures
of rainbows.

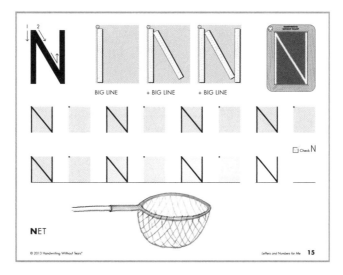

OBJECTIVE: To write capital **N** with correct formation.

Lesson Plan
Let's find the capital N page. Help children turn to p. 15. Discuss what's on the page.

1. Demonstrate
Demonstrate **N** on the Slate Chalkboard, whiteboard, or flip chart.
Use Capitals on the Door for **N** (multisensory activity p. 64).
Children finger trace the large capital **N** model in their workbooks.

2. Copy
Prepare for writing with good posture, pencil grip, and use of the helper hand.
Demonstrate **N** again, saying the step-by-step directions together.
Children watch, then copy **N**'s.

3. Check & Evaluate
Help children ☑ their letter for correct Start, Steps, and Bump.
Evaluate the correct formation for capital **N**.

Read, Color & Draw
Read the word NET together. Point out the beginning of capital **N**.
Encourage free coloring and drawing. Add something in the net, water, etc.

More to Learn
Use "Diagonals," track 5, *Rock, Rap, Tap & Learn* CD.
While standing, make the diagonal motion in the air.
Show children what diagonal looks like in the letter **N**.

Support/ELL
If a child makes the diagonal stroke incorrectly, like starting
at the bottom of the first line, play the Mystery Letters on
the Slate Chalkboard or Gray Blocks (p. 60).

CONNECTIONS

Math Link: Bring in a net. Have children go on a
scavenger hunt and collect things in their net (leaves,
rocks, sticks, etc.). Sort items by length and discuss.

M

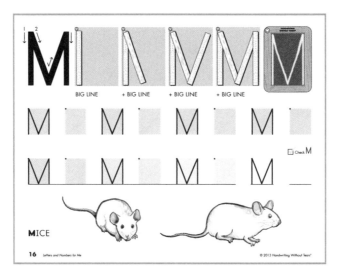

OBJECTIVE: To write capital **M** with correct formation.

Lesson Plan
Let's find the capital M page. Help children turn to p. 16. Discuss what's on the page.

1. Demonstrate
Demonstrate **M** on the Slate Chalkboard, whiteboard, or flip chart.
Use Capitals on the Door for **M** (multisensory activity p. 64).
Children finger trace the large capital **M** model in their workbooks.

2. Copy
Prepare for writing with good posture, pencil grip, and use of the helper hand.
Demonstrate **M** again, saying the step-by-step directions together.
Children watch, then copy **M**'s.

3. Check & Evaluate
Help children ☑ their letter for correct Start, Steps, and Bump.
Evaluate the correct formation for capital **M**.

Read, Color & Draw
Read the word MICE together. Point out the beginning of capital **M**.
Encourage free coloring and drawing. Add cheese, grass, etc.

More to Learn
Use "Diagonals," track 5, *Rock, Rap, Tap & Learn* CD.
While standing, make the diagonal motion in the air.
Show children what a diagonal looks like in the letter **M**.

Support/ELL
Some children find it helpful to think of making a **V** after the first Big Line. Say the word "diagonal" as children are making these strokes in the letter **M**.

CONNECTIONS

Language Arts Link: Read *If You Give a Mouse a Cookie* by Laura Joffe Numeroff. Discuss the difference between a real mouse and the mouse in the story.

OBJECTIVE: To review and write Frog Jump Capitals with correct formation.

Lesson Plan

Help children turn to p. 17. Say the letters **F**, **E**, **D**, **P**, **B**, **R**, **N**, and **M** together. Ask children what is said after a Big Line is made. Children will respond "Ribbit" to indicate the Frog Jump or return to the Starting Corner.

1. **Copy the Frog Jump Capitals.**
   Here are all the Frog Jump Capitals. Get ready to copy F. Put your pencil on the dot (Starting Corner). Now make: Big Line down, Frog Jump! Ribbit! Little Line across the top, Little Line across the middle. Repeat for **E**, **D**, **P**, **B**, **R**, **N**, and **M**.

2. **Play the Mystery Letter Game.**
   Now let's play the Mystery Letter game with Frog Jump Capitals.
   Put your pencil on the dot (Starting Corner).
   Make a Big Line down.
   Frog Jump back to the dot (Starting Corner). Wait.
   Make letter **B** (or **N**, **P**, **E**, **F**, **M**, **R**, and **D**, etc.).

3. **Check & Evaluate**
   Evaluate children's letter formations to be sure they are playing the game correctly and avoiding reversals.

More to Learn

Use "Frog Jump Letters," track 12, *Rock, Rap, Tap & Learn* CD. While standing, finger trace Frog Jump Capitals in the air. Let children jump between singing the verses.

Support/ELL

Have students say the directions out loud. Children like to say "Ribbit" for the Frog Jump. Demonstrate the movement of the jump from the bottom of the Big Line to the top.

CONNECTIONS

▶ **Video Lesson:** View "Teaching Frog Jump Capitals" at **hwtears.com/videos**

🏠 **Home Link:** This is the end of the Frog Jump Capitals group. A description of these letters and home practice is available at **hwtears.com/click**

H

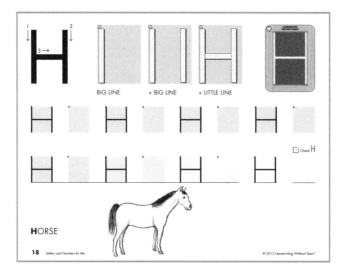

OBJECTIVE: To write capital **H** with correct formation.

Lesson Plan
Let's find the capital H page. Help children turn to p. 18. Discuss what's on the page.

1. Demonstrate
Demonstrate **H** on the Slate Chalkboard, whiteboard, or flip chart.
Use "Give It A Middle," track 13, *Rock, Rap, Tap & Learn* CD.
Children finger trace the large capital **H** model in their workbooks.

2. Copy
Prepare for writing with good posture, pencil grip, and use of the helper hand.
Demonstrate **H** again, saying the step-by-step directions together.
Children watch, then copy **H**'s.

3. Check & Evaluate
Help children ☑ their letter for correct Start, Steps, and Bump.
Evaluate the correct formation for capital **H**.

Read, Color & Draw
Read the word HORSE together. Point out the beginning of capital **H**.
Encourage free coloring and drawing. Add hay, grass, etc.

More to Learn
Build **H** using Show Me Magnetic Pieces for Capitals™ (p. 58).
Hold up a picture of lowercase **h** next to the capital. Discuss
that some capitals are different from their lowercase partners.

Support/ELL
Capital **H** does not Frog Jump back to the Starting Corner.
Remember left-handed students can write cross strokes
from right to left pulling into their hand.

CONNECTIONS

Math Link: Bring in a toy horse. Have children count
how many legs, mouth, nose, ears, tails, feet, etc.

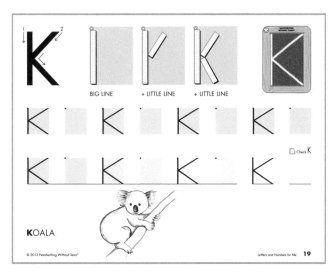

OBJECTIVE: To write capital **K** with correct formation.

Lesson Plan
Let's find the capital K page. Help children turn to p. 19. Discuss what's on the page.

1. Demonstrate
Demonstrate **K** on the Slate Chalkboard, whiteboard, or flip chart.
Use Letter Story for **K** (multisensory activity p. 106).
Children finger trace the large capital **K** model in their workbooks.

2. Copy
Prepare for writing with good posture, pencil grip, and use of the helper hand.
Demonstrate **K** again, saying the step-by-step directions together.
Children watch, then copy **K**'s.

3. Check & Evaluate
Help children ✓ their letter for correct Start, Steps, and Bump.
Evaluate the correct formation for capital **K**.

Read, Color & Draw
Read the word KOALA together. Point out the beginning of capital **K**.
Encourage free coloring and drawing. Add leaves, sun, etc.

More to Learn
Build **K** using Show Me Magnetic Pieces for Capitals™
(p. 58). Hold up a picture of lowercase **k** next to the capital.
Discuss that the lowercase partner has a lower kick.

Support/ELL
This style of **K** uses only two strokes. Help children start the
second stroke in the top right corner, and kick in one stroke
to end in the bottom right.

CONNECTIONS

Social Studies Link: Read about Australia. Not only
will students learn about koalas, they can learn another
native Australian animal that begins with **K**—kangaroo.

BIG LINE   + LITTLE LINE

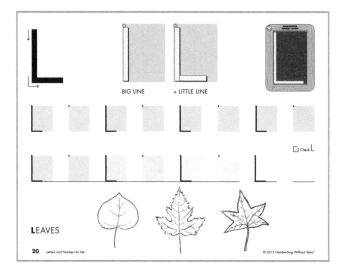

OBJECTIVE: To write capital **L** with correct formation.

Lesson Plan
Let's find the capital L page. Help children turn to p. 20. Discuss what's on the page.

1. Demonstrate
Demonstrate **L** on the Slate Chalkboard, whiteboard, or flip chart.
Use Air Writing for **L** (multisensory activity p. 61).
Children finger trace the large capital **L** model in their workbooks.

2. Copy
Prepare for writing with good posture, pencil grip, and use of the helper hand.
Demonstrate **L** again, saying the step-by-step directions together.
Children watch, then copy **L**'s.

3. Check & Evaluate
Help children ☑ their letter for correct Start, Steps, and Bump.
Evaluate the correct formation for capital **L**.

Read, Color & Draw
Read the word LEAVES together. Point out the beginning of capital **L**.
Encourage free coloring and drawing. Add more leaves, a tree, etc.

More to Learn
Find **L** in the alphabet. Ask children if **L** is in the beginning, middle, or end of the alphabet. What letter is before **L**? After **L**?

Support/ELL
Letter **L** uses just one continuous stroke, so encourage children to keep their pencil on the page as they hit the corner and begin to write the Little Line.

CONNECTIONS

Science Link: Bring in real leaves or go on a hunt for leaves around the school. Discuss the similarities and differences. Classify leaves by shape, size, texture, color, or type.

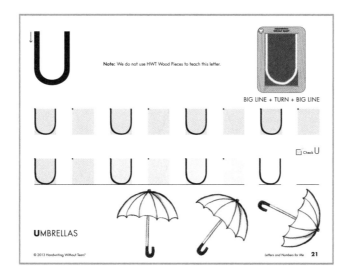

OBJECTIVE: To write capital **U** with correct formation.

Lesson Plan
Let's find the capital U page. Help children turn to p. 21. Discuss what's on the page.

1. Demonstrate
Demonstrate **U** on the Slate Chalkboard, whiteboard, or flip chart.
Use Laser Letters for **U** (multisensory activity p. 62).
Children finger trace the large capital **U** model in their workbooks.

2. Copy
Prepare for writing with good posture, pencil grip, and use of the helper hand.
Demonstrate **U** again, saying the step-by-step directions together.
Children watch, then copy **U**'s.

3. Check & Evaluate
Help children ☑ their letter for correct Start, Steps, and Bump.
Evaluate the correct formation for capital **U**.

Read, Color & Draw
Read the word UMBRELLAS together. Point out the beginning of capital **U**.
Encourage free coloring and drawing. Add raindrops, clouds, etc.

More to Learn
Review vocabulary concepts of open/close. Bring in an umbrella from home and show children how it opens and closes. Say the words out loud as a class.

Support/ELL
Do not make **U** with Wood Pieces because it ends up an odd shape and size. Instead tell a story: **U** go down, **U** walk on the bottom, and **U** go up.

CONNECTIONS

Social Studies Link: Show children a map of places in the world where it rains the most (i.e., Mount Waialeale, Hawaii or Cherrapunji, India).

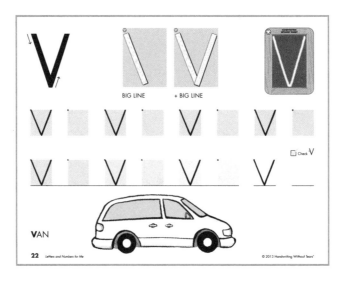

OBJECTIVE: To write capital **V** with correct formation.

Lesson Plan
Let's find the capital V page. Help children turn to p. 22. Discuss what's on the page.

1. **Demonstrate**
   Demonstrate **V** on the Slate Chalkboard, whiteboard, or flip chart.
   Use "Sliding Down to the End of the Alphabet," track 15, *Rock, Rap, Tap & Learn* CD.
   Children finger trace the large capital **V** model in their workbooks.

2. **Copy**
   Prepare for writing with good posture, pencil grip, and use of the helper hand.
   Demonstrate **V** again, saying the step-by-step directions together.
   Children watch, then copy **V**'s.

3. **Check & Evaluate**
   Help children ☑ their letter for correct Start, Steps, and Bump.
   Evaluate the correct formation for capital **V**.

Read, Color & Draw
Read the word VAN together. Point out the beginning of capital **V**.
Encourage free coloring and drawing. Add a road, passengers in the van, etc.

More to Learn
Use Wood Pieces to make a **V**. Each child gets two Big Lines to hold together at the bottom and then open—"Voilà!" Review words top, bottom, and open.

Support/ELL
Show children how **V** needs to have a very sharp point at the bottom or people will think it's a **U**. Make fingers into **V**'s.

CONNECTIONS

▶ **Video Lesson:** View "Sliding Down to the End of the Alphabet" at **hwtears.com/videos**

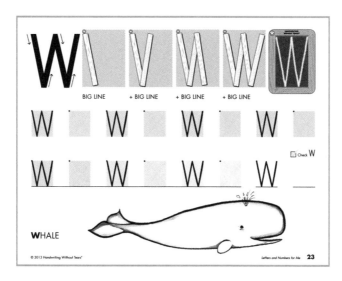

WHALE

OBJECTIVE: To write capital **W** with correct formation.

Lesson Plan
Let's find the capital W page. Help children turn to p. 23. Discuss what's on the page.

1. Demonstrate
Demonstrate **W** on the Slate Chalkboard, whiteboard, or flip chart.
Use "Diagonals," track 5, *Rock, Rap, Tap & Learn* CD.
Children finger trace the large capital **W** model in their workbooks.

2. Copy
Prepare for writing with good posture, pencil grip, and use of the helper hand.
Demonstrate **W** again, saying the step-by-step directions together.
Children watch, then copy **W**'s.

3. Check & Evaluate
Help children ☑ their letter for correct Start, Steps, and Bump.
Evaluate the correct formation for capital **W**.

Read, Color & Draw
Read the word WHALE together. Point out the beginning of capital **W**.
Encourage free coloring and drawing. Add water, small fish, etc.

More to Learn

Find **W** in the alphabet. Ask children if **W** is in the beginning, middle, or end of the alphabet. What letter is before **W**? After **W**?

Support/ELL

Use Wood Pieces to make **V**. Each child gets two Big Lines to hold together at the bottom and then open. Children hold **V**'s together to make **W**. Review words: apart and together.

CONNECTIONS

Science Link: Discuss whales. Bring in pictures of other animals. Using a Venn diagram, compare and contrast animals that live in water and animals that live on land.

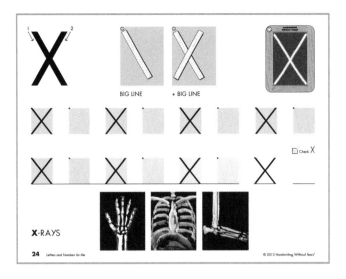

OBJECTIVE: To write capital **X** with correct formation.

Lesson Plan
Let's find the capital X page. Help children turn to p. 24. Discuss what's on the page.

1. Demonstrate
Demonstrate **X** on the Slate Chalkboard, whiteboard, or flip chart.
Use Laser Letters for **X** (multisensory activity p. 62).
Children finger trace the large capital **X** model in their workbooks.

2. Copy
Prepare for writing with good posture, pencil grip, and use of the helper hand.
Demonstrate **X** again, saying the step-by-step directions together.
Children watch, then copy **X**'s.

3. Check & Evaluate
Help children ☑ their letter for correct Start, Steps, and Bump.
Evaluate the correct formation for capital **X**.

Read, Color & Draw
Read the word X-RAYS together. Point out the beginning of capital **X**.
Encourage free coloring and drawing. Add more bones.

More to Learn
Use "Sliding Down to the End of the Alphabet," track 15, *Rock, Rap, Tap & Learn* CD to Air Write **X** and review **V** and **W**.

Support/ELL
Use two Wood Pieces (Big Lines) to make an **X** in the air.
Tap the Big Lines together in the middle and say, "**X** marks the spot." Review diagonals with Big Lines (pp. 38–39).

CONNECTIONS

Science Link: Discuss X-rays. Why do we need them? What do they show? Discuss the pictures in the workbook.

Y

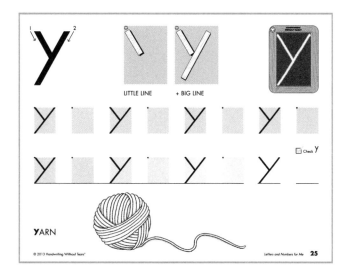

YARN

© 2013 Handwriting Without Tears®   Letters and Numbers for Me **25**

OBJECTIVE: To write capital **Y** with correct formation.

Lesson Plan
Let's find the capital Y page. Help children turn to p. 25. Discuss what's on the page.

1. **Demonstrate**
   Demonstrate **Y** on the Slate Chalkboard, whiteboard, or flip chart.
   Use "My Teacher Writes," track 21, *Rock, Rap, Tap & Learn* CD.
   Children finger trace the large capital **Y** model in their workbooks.

2. **Copy**
   Prepare for writing with good posture, pencil grip, and use of the helper hand.
   Demonstrate **Y** again, saying the step-by-step directions together.
   Children watch, then copy **Y**'s.

3. **Check & Evaluate**
   Help children ☑ their letter for correct Start, Steps, and Bump.
   Evaluate the correct formation for capital **Y**.

Read, Color & Draw
Read the word YARN together. Point out the beginning of capital **Y**.
Encourage free coloring and drawing. Add another ball of yarn, make yarn longer, etc.

More to Learn
Use "Sliding Down to the End of the Alphabet," track 15,
Rock, Rap, Tap & Learn CD to air write **Y** and review **V**, **W**,
X, and **Y**.

Support/ELL
Diagonals strokes can be difficult. Demonstrate in the air.
Use "Diagonals," track 5, *Rock, Rap, Tap & Learn* CD.
Show what diagonals look like in letter **Y**.

CONNECTIONS

Math Link: Use yarn as a non-standard measurement
tool. Children can measure two different items and
compare which is longer and which is shorter.

Z

LITTLE LINE   + BIG LINE   + LITTLE LINE

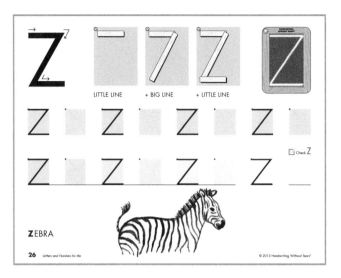

OBJECTIVE: To write capital **Z** with correct formation.

Lesson Plan

Let's find the capital Z page. Help children turn to p. 26. Discuss what's on the page.

1. Demonstrate

Demonstrate **Z** on the Slate Chalkboard, whiteboard, or flip chart.
Use "Sliding Down to the End of the Alphabet," track 15, *Rock, Rap, Tap & Learn* CD.
Children finger trace the large capital **Z** model in their workbooks.

2. Copy

Prepare for writing with good posture, pencil grip, and use of the helper hand.
Demonstrate **Z** again, saying the step-by-step directions together.
Children watch, then copy **Z**'s.

3. Check & Evaluate

Help children ☑ their letter for correct Start, Steps, and Bump.
Evaluate the correct formation for capital **Z**.

Read, Color & Draw

Read the word ZEBRA together. Point out the beginning of capital **Z**.
Encourage free coloring and drawing. Add other animals, grass, etc.

More to Learn

Z is the last letter in the alphabet. Help children find letters in the beginning, middle, and end of the alphabet.

Support/ELL

Z can be reversed. Practice writing **Z** by using the Slate Chalkboard and Wet-Dry-Try (p. 59). The Starting Corner prevents the reversals.

CONNECTIONS

▶ **Video Lesson:** View "Sliding Down to the End of the Alphabet" at **hwtears.com/videos**

🏠 **Home Link:** This is the end of the Starting Corner Capitals group. A description of these letters and home practice is available at **hwtears.com/click**

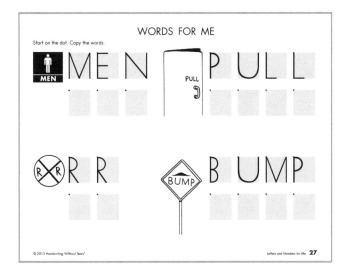

OBJECTIVE: To practice writing capitals using common signs in the community.

Lesson Plan

Help children turn to p. 27. Discuss what's on the page.

1. Demonstrate & Copy

Gather the Slate Chalkboard and chalk to demonstrate letters.
Demonstrate **M** on the Slate Chalkboard with step-by-step directions.
Children copy **M** in their books.
Repeat directions letter by letter for each word. Use Frog Jump terminology where appropriate.

2. Check & Evaluate

Evaluate children as they copy the words and help as needed.

Read & Color

Read the words MEN, PULL, RR (abbreviation), and BUMP together.
Encourage free coloring.

More to Learn

Discuss the pictures. Explain that two are building signs and two are road signs. Discuss the meaning of all the words.

Support/ELL

When the word is a verb, act out the meaning. Show children bathroom signs. Show children a picture of a real RR crossing.

CONNECTIONS

Social Studies Link: Have children color the signs and discuss their importance to the community. Download other community signs from **hwtears.com/click**

OBJECTIVE: To write capital **C** with correct formation.

Lesson Plan

Let's find the capital C page. Help children turn to p. 28. Discuss what's on the page.

1. Demonstrate

Demonstrate **C** on the Slate Chalkboard, whiteboard, or flip chart.
Use Capitals on the Door for **C** (multisensory activity p. 64).
Children finger trace the large capital **C** model in their workbooks.

2. Copy

Prepare for writing with good posture, pencil grip, and use of the helper hand.
Demonstrate **C** again, saying the step-by-step directions together.
Children watch, then copy **C**'s.

3. Check & Evaluate

Help children ☑ their letter for correct Start, Steps, and Bump.
Evaluate the correct formation for capital **C**.

Read, Color & Draw

Read the word CAR together. Point out the beginning of capital **C**.
Encourage free coloring and drawing. Add a road, passengers in the car, etc.

More to Learn

Make your own Magic C Bunny Puppet (p. 188). It's simple and all you need is a napkin and a marker.

Support/ELL

C is a Center Starting Capital. Show children the top center of the door or the Slate Chalkboard and say "center." Tell children to travel towards the smiley face.

CONNECTIONS

Social Studies Link: Discuss the car. Identify types of transportation and look at pictures. Have children identify non-motorized transportation.

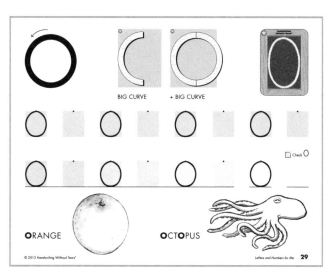

OBJECTIVE: To write capital O with correct formation.

Lesson Plan
Let's find the capital O page. Help children turn to p. 29. Discuss what's on the page.

1. Demonstrate
Demonstrate O on the Slate Chalkboard, whiteboard, or flip chart.
Use Laser Letters for O (multisensory activity p. 62).
Children finger trace the large capital O model in their workbooks.

2. Copy
Prepare for writing with good posture, pencil grip, and use of the helper hand.
Demonstrate O again, saying the step-by-step directions together.
Children watch, then copy O's.

3. Check & Evaluate
Help children ✓ their letter for correct Start, Steps, and Bump.
Evaluate the correct formation for capital O.

Read, Color & Draw
Read the words ORANGE and OCTOPUS together. Point out the beginning of capital O's and the next O. Encourage free coloring and drawing. Add other fruit, a baby octopus, etc.

More to Learn
Show children that the symbol O works as a letter, a shape (circle) and a number (zero). They all begin with Magic C. Make O's with your mouth.

Support/ELL
Slowly repeat the step-by-step directions, exactly as they appear. Help left-handed children begin O with Magic C. Left-handed children are more likely to begin letter O incorrectly.

CONNECTIONS

Science Link: Discuss the ocean and where octopuses live. Discuss other animals that live in the ocean. Make a class list.

Q

BIG CURVE   + BIG CURVE   + LITTLE LINE

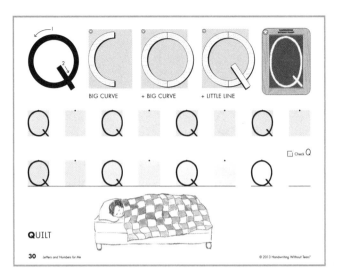

BIG CURVE   + BIG CURVE   + LITTLE LINE

☐ Check Q

QUILT

30 Letters and Numbers for Me   © 2013 Handwriting Without Tears®

OBJECTIVE: To write capital **Q** with correct formation.

Lesson Plan
Let's find the capital Q page. Help children turn to p. 30. Discuss what's on the page.

1. **Demonstrate**
   Demonstrate **Q** on the Slate Chalkboard, whiteboard, or flip chart.
   Use Laser Letters for **Q** (multisensory activity p. 62).
   Children finger trace the large capital **Q** model in their workbooks.

2. **Copy**
   Prepare for writing with good posture, pencil grip, and use of the helper hand.
   Demonstrate **Q** again, saying the step-by-step directions together.
   Children watch, then copy **Q**'s.

3. **Check & Evaluate**
   Help children ☑ their letter for correct Start, Steps, and Bump.
   Evaluate the correct formation for capital **Q**.

Read, Color & Draw
Read the word QUILT together. Point out the beginning of capital **Q**.
Encourage free coloring and drawing. Add color patterns to quilt.

More to Learn
Find **Q** in the alphabet. Help children identify letters before
and after **Q**.

Support/ELL
If children forget which direction to go, get the Slate
Chalkboard out and tell them to travel towards the smiley
face. Tell children that **Q** is like an **O** with a Little Line.

CONNECTIONS

Math Link: Bring in a real quilt or pictures of quilts.
Look at patterns in quilts. Compare quilt sizes
(big and small).

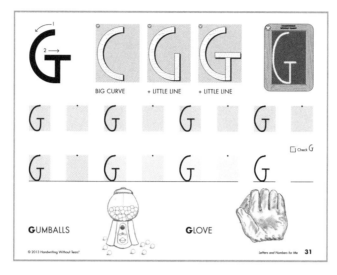

OBJECTIVE: To write capital **G** with correct formation.

Lesson Plan
Let's find the capital G page. Help children turn to p. 31. Discuss what's on the page.

1. Demonstrate
Demonstrate **G** on the Slate Chalkboard, whiteboard, or flip chart.
Use Laser Letters for **G** (multisensory activity p. 62).
Children finger trace the large capital **G** model in their workbooks.

2. Copy
Prepare for writing with good posture, pencil grip, and use of the helper hand.
Demonstrate **G** again, saying the step-by-step directions together.
Children watch, then copy **G**'s.

3. Check & Evaluate
Help children ☑ their letter for correct Start, Steps, and Bump.
Evaluate the correct formation for capital **G**.

Read, Color & Draw
Read the words GUMBALLS and GLOVE together. Point out the beginning of capital **G**'s.
Encourage free coloring and drawing. Add more gumballs, a baseball in the glove, etc.

More to Learn
Review ☑ Check letter: Start, Steps, and Bump. See p. 67 of this teacher's guide.

Support/ELL
To reinforce the Center Starting Capitals and correct formation habits for Magic C Capitals, play the Mystery Letters on the Slate Chalkboard or on Gray Blocks (p. 60).

CONNECTIONS

Language Arts Link: Discuss compound words. Gumball is a compound word. Help children hear the two words. Make a class list of other compound words.

Math Link: Bring in other types of gloves. Line them up. Have children count the total number of fingers on the gloves.

Magic C Capitals

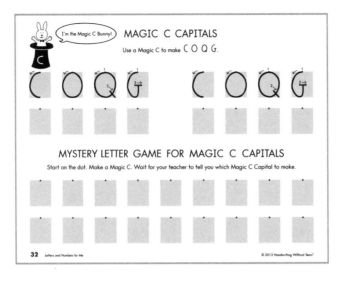

OBJECTIVE: To review and write Magic C Capitals with correct formation.

Lesson Plan

Help children turn to p. 32. Say the letters **C, O, Q,** and **G** together. Remind students about the Magic C Bunny.

1. **Copy the Magic C Capitals.**
   Here are the Magic C Capitals on one page. Get ready to copy C. Put your pencil on the dot. Now make: Magic C. Repeat for **O, G,** and **Q.**

2. **Play the Mystery Letter Game.**
   Now let's play the Mystery Letter Game for Magic C Capitals.
   Put your pencil on the dot. Magic C.
   Make a letter O (or **G, Q,** and **C**)**.**

3. **Check & Evaluate**
   Check children's letter formations to be sure they play the game correctly and avoid reversals.

More to Learn

Play Guess My Letter. Say, "Magic C, keep going." Children respond, "**O.**" Say, "Magic C, Little Line up, Little Line across." Children respond, "**G.**"

Support/ELL

You may choose to mark the top center of the Slate Chalkboard (or the door) with a small mark to orient children to the center.

CONNECTIONS

🏠 **Home Link:** This is the end of the Magic C Capitals group. A description of these letters and home practice is available at **hwtears.com/click**

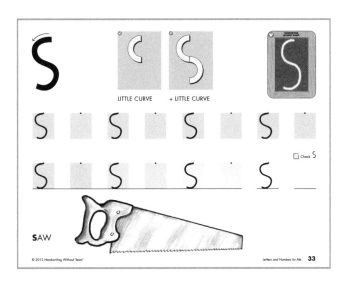

OBJECTIVE: To write capital **S** with correct formation.

Lesson Plan
Let's find the capital S page. Help children turn to p. 33. Discuss what's on the page.

1. Demonstrate
Demonstrate **S** on the Slate Chalkboard, whiteboard, or flip chart.
Use "My Teacher Writes," track 21, *Rock, Rap, Tap & Learn* CD.
Children finger trace the large capital **S** model in their workbooks.

2. Copy
Prepare for writing with good posture, pencil grip, and use of the helper hand.
Demonstrate **S** again, saying the step-by-step directions together.
Children watch, then copy **S**'s.

3. Check & Evaluate
Help children ☑ their letter for correct Start, Steps, and Bump.
Evaluate the correct formation for capital **S**.

Read, Color & Draw
Read the word SAW together. Point out the beginning of capital **S**.
Encourage free coloring and drawing. Add wood, more tools, etc.

More to Learn
Teach **S** and review **C**, **O**, **V**, and **W** with "CAPITALS & lowercase," track 16, R*ock, Rap, Tap & Learn* CD.

Support/ELL
S starts in the center. Show children the center of the door or the Slate Chalkboard and say "center." If children forget which direction to go, tell them to travel towards the smiley face.

CONNECTIONS

Language Arts Link: A saw is a tool used for cutting wood. Talk about the word "saw" as a verb. Make the motions of sawing wood.

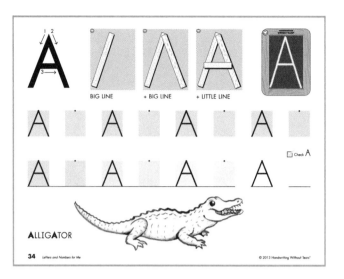

OBJECTIVE: To write capital **A** with correct formation.

Lesson Plan
Let's find the capital A page. Help children turn to p. 34. Discuss what's on the page.

1. Demonstrate
Demonstrate **A** on the Slate Chalkboard, whiteboard, or flip chart.
Use "Give It A Middle," track 13, *Rock, Rap, Tap & Learn* CD.
Children finger trace the large capital **A** model in their workbooks.

2. Copy
Prepare for writing with good posture, pencil grip, and use of the helper hand.
Demonstrate **A** again, saying the step-by-step directions together.
Children watch, then copy **A**'s.

3. Check & Evaluate
Help children ☑ their letter for correct Start, Steps, and Bump.
Evaluate the correct formation for capital **A**.

Read, Color & Draw
Read the word ALLIGATOR together. Point out the beginning of capital **A** and the next **A**.
Encourage free coloring and drawing. Add water, dirt, etc.

More to Learn
Build **A** using Show Me Magnetic Pieces for Capitals™ (p. 58).
Hold up a picture of a lowercase **a** next to the capital. Discuss
that some capitals are different from their lowercase partners.

Support/ELL
Teach that **A** starts in the center. Remember left-handed
students can write cross strokes from right to left pulling into
their hand. Review diagonal strokes.

CONNECTIONS

Science Link: Read the *Yucky Reptile Alphabet Book* by
Jerry Pallotta. Discuss the reptiles in the books. Make a
list of reptile features.

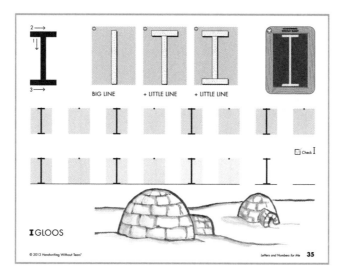

OBJECTIVE: To write capital **I** with correct formation.

Lesson Plan
Let's find the capital I page. Help children turn to p. 35. Discuss what's on the page.

1. Demonstrate
Demonstrate **I** on the Slate Chalkboard, whiteboard, or flip chart.
Use "Give It A Top," track 14, *Rock, Rap, Tap & Learn* CD.
Children finger trace the large capital **I** model in their workbooks.

2. Copy
Prepare for writing with good posture, pencil grip, and use of the helper hand.
Demonstrate **I** again, saying the step-by-step directions together.
Children watch, then copy **I**'s.

3. Check & Evaluate
Help children ☑ their letter for correct Start, Steps, and Bump.
Evaluate the correct formation for capital **I**.

Read, Color & Draw
Read the word IGLOOS together. Point out the beginning of capital **I**.
Encourage free coloring and drawing. Add people, snowflakes, etc.

More to Learn
Show children that **I** is different from l because it has a top and bottom. Use a Big Line from the Wood Pieces to review top and bottom.

Support/ELL
Remember left-handed children can write cross strokes right to left. Review top and bottom by building **I** with Show Me Magnetic Pieces for Capitals™.

CONNECTIONS

Social Studies Link: Discuss igloos and where they are built. Show children pictures of igloos. Compare and contrast an igloo and a house.

BIG LINE   + LITTLE LINE

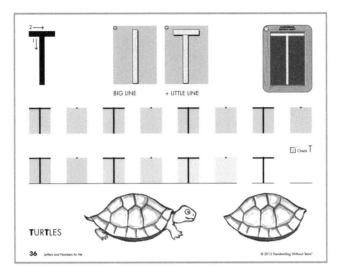

OBJECTIVE: To write capital **T** with correct formation.

Lesson Plan
Let's find the capital T page. Help children turn to p. 36. Discuss what's on the page.

1. Demonstrate
Demonstrate **T** on the Slate Chalkboard, whiteboard, or flip chart.
Use "Give It A Top," track 14, *Rock, Rap, Tap & Learn* CD.
Children finger trace the large capital **T** model in their workbooks.

2. Copy
Prepare for writing with good posture, pencil grip, and use of the helper hand.
Demonstrate **T** again, saying the step-by-step directions together.
Children watch, then copy **T**'s.

3. Check & Evaluate
Help children ☑ their letter for correct Start, Steps, and Bump.
Evaluate the correct formation for capital **T**.

Read, Color & Draw
Read the word TURTLES together. Point out the beginning of capital **T** and the next **T**.
Encourage free coloring and drawing. Add water, dirt, etc.

More to Learn
Look at the picture of the turtles. Discuss the concepts of in and out. Discuss why turtles might go "in" their shells.

Support/ELL
To teach children the difference between capital **T** and lowercase **t**, use Letter Story for **T** and **t** (p. 107).

CONNECTIONS

Language Arts Link: Write a class story about a turtle. Be sure to name the turtle something that starts with the letter **T**. Circle all **T**'s in the story when finished.

Science Link: Discuss turtles. Look at informational books about turtles. Make a class list of things related to turtles.

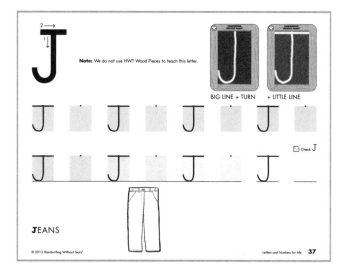

OBJECTIVE: To write capital **J** with correct formation.

Lesson Plan
Let's find the capital J page. Help children turn to p. 37. Discuss what's on the page.

1. **Demonstrate**
   Demonstrate **J** on the Slate Chalkboard, whiteboard, or flip chart.
   Use "Give It A Top," track 14, *Rock, Rap, Tap & Learn* CD.
   Children finger trace the large capital **J** model in their workbooks.

2. **Copy**
   Prepare for writing with good posture, pencil grip, and use of the helper hand.
   Demonstrate **J** again, saying the step-by-step directions together.
   Children watch, then copy **J**'s.

3. **Check & Evaluate**
   Help children ☑ their letter for correct Start, Steps, and Bump.
   Evaluate the correct formation for capital **J**.

Read, Color & Draw
Read the word JEANS together. Point out the beginning of capital **J**.
Encourage free coloring and drawing. Add a shirt, socks, etc.

More to Learn
Demonstrate **J** on the Slate Chalkboard. Hold up a lowercase **j** next to the capital. Discuss that some capitals are different from their lowercase partner.

Support/ELL
Review top by demonstrating **J** on the Slate Chalkboard. Invite children to finger trace Little Line at the top. Remember left-handed children can write cross strokes right to left.

CONNECTIONS

🏠 **Home Link:** This is the end of the Center Starting Capitals group. A description of these letters and home practice is available at **hwtears.com/click**

Words for Me

OBJECTIVE: To practice writing capitals using common signs in the community.

Lesson Plan
Help children turn to p. 38. Discuss what's on the page.

1. Demonstrate and copy the words.
Gather the Slate Chalkboard, chalk, and paper towel to demonstrate letters.
Demonstrate **S** on the Slate Chalkboard with step-by-step directions.
Children copy **S** in their book.
Repeat directions letter by letter for each word.

2. Check & Evaluate
Evaluate children as they copy the words, and help them as needed.

Read & Color
Read the words STOP, WALK, GIRLS, and BUS together.
Encourage free coloring.

More to Learn
Go on a "sign" hunt around the school. Make a list and discuss important signs found.

Support/ELL
When the word is a verb, act out the meaning. Have children walk, then hold up a stop sign and have them stop. Show children bathroom signs.

CONNECTIONS

Social Studies Link: Discuss the pictures. Explain the importance of signs in our community (safety, location). Discuss the bus and different types of transportation.

Capitals for Me

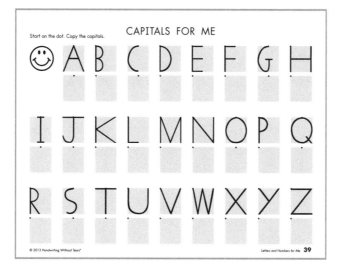

OBJECTIVE: To practice writing all capitals correctly.

Lesson Plan

Help children turn to p. 39. Say all the capitals in the alphabet together.

1. **Prepare to write all of the capitals.**
   Sing the alphabet and have children point to the letters as they sing.
   Prepare for writing with good posture, pencil grip, and use of the helper hand.

2. **Copy the capitals.**
   Find A. Get ready to copy A in the Gray Block.
   Put your pencil on the dot.
   Big Line slides down, jump to the dot.
   Big Line slides down,
   Little Line across.
   Complete the rest of letters, saying the step-by-step directions for each letter.

   Note: You may decide to do just one row a day.

3. **Check & Evaluate**
   Evaluate children as they copy the letters, and help them as needed.

More to Learn

Once the page is complete, celebrate by dancing and singing the "Alphabet Boogie," track 1, *Rock, Rap, Tap & Learn* CD.

Support/ELL

When you point and sing, it helps children to associate a letter name with the letter symbol. If a child is having difficulty forming a letter, model on the Slate Chalkboard.

CONNECTIONS

Home Link: Have children do an "Alphabet Show & Tell." A description of this activity is available at **hwtears.com/click**

LOWERCASE LETTERS,
Words, Sentences & More

It's time for all the letters, words, and sentences. The 26 capitals you've taught already give your students an excellent start for lowercase letters. Lowercase lessons begin with letters your students already know. We start with **c**, **o**, **s**, **v**, and **w**—five letters that are exactly the same as capitals just smaller. That's not all. Beginning with those five letters gives another opportunity for you to be sure every child has good habits for **c**, **o**, **s**, **v**, and **w**. That's an excellent lowercase start.

Words come next. As soon as children know **c**, **o**, **s**, **v**, **w** and letter **t**, they're writing words. Handwriting Without Tears® word practice is different. It's deliberately designed to promote correct letter formation and writing fluency. Our words avoid untaught letters. We select words with only the letters that children have been carefully taught to write correctly.

Because only familiar and previously taught letters are used in our word practice, children typically use correct habits for writing every letter. With word practice, those habits become automatic and lead directly to fluency. At first, every new letter takes care and conscious effort, but gradually, more letters are written both correctly and automatically.

Sentences follow words. As soon as children know three more lowercase letters: **a**, **d**, and **g**, they begin sentences. We teach the basics (capital, spacing, ending punctuation) with "Sentence Song." We carefully plan for sentence spacing. We know that when sentences are poorly modeled with skimpy spaces, children struggle with correct spacing. That's why we give kindergartners very generous spaces (two fingers!) and we plan for this.

With letter, word, and sentence skills well in hand, we introduce children to fuller written expression with activity pages. Enjoy giving your students a taste of rhyming, poetry, punctuation marks, paragraphs, and even quotations.

Lowercase Teaching Order

Our lowercase teaching order promotes success:

1. Good habits for letter formation: All lowercase letters (except **d** and **e**) begin at the top.
2. Correct placement: The tall, small, and descending letters are in proportion and placed correctly.
3. Correct orientation: No **b** and **d** confusion, no **g** and **q** confusion, no reversed letters!

Lowercase Letters Are Taught in Five Groups

Same as Capitals & t

c o s v w   t

Magic c

a d g

Transition Group

u i e l k y j

Diver Letters

p r n m h b

Final Group

f q x z

The first five letters are exactly like their capitals, just smaller. What an easy start—just bring your good habits from capitals! Lowercase **t** is made like **T**. It's just crossed lower.

These high frequency letters begin with the familiar Magic c. Starting with **c** placed correctly helps children make and place the **d** tall and **g** descending.

Here are the rest of the vowels: **u**, **i**, **e**. Letters **u**, **k**, **y**, **j** are familiar from capitals. The focus will be on careful placement and size.

These letters all start with the same pattern: they dive down, swim up, swim over! We avoid **b** and **d** confusion by separating the letters and teaching them in different groups based on formation habits.

Lowercase **f** has a tricky start. Letter **q** is taught here to avoid **g** and **q** confusion. Letters **x** and **z** are familiar, but infrequently used.

Lowercase Letter Frequency

In 1948, Dr. Edward Dolch published a list of 220 high frequency words (Dolch 1948). He had word lists for preprimer, primer, first, second, and third grade. To identify high frequency printed words for grades K–2, we used the 177 words on the lists through second grade. Then, we counted how often each letter appears to determine individual letter frequency. This chart shows the letters in order of decreasing frequency. This information shaped our teaching order. You can use this chart to make priority decisions about correcting or reviewing letters.

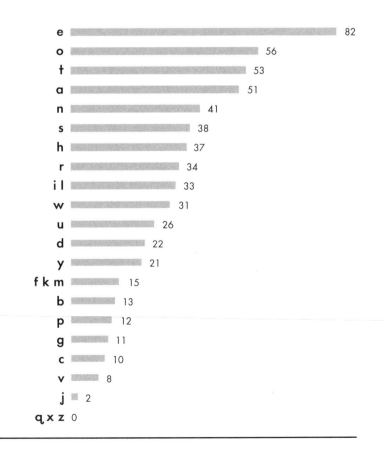

Letter	Frequency
e	82
o	56
t	53
a	51
n	41
s	38
h	37
r	34
i l	33
w	31
u	26
d	22
y	21
f k m	15
b	13
p	12
g	11
c	10
v	8
j	2
q x z	0

At the board and in the workbook, the focus of your teaching will be on letters, words, and sentences. You are teaching letter formation as well as word and sentence skills. You will teach in easy, small steps so your students know exactly what to do. Then, you'll help them develop their ability to ☑ letter, word, and sentence skills. Use p. 5 of *Letters and Numbers for Me* to explain what is expected when they self-check.

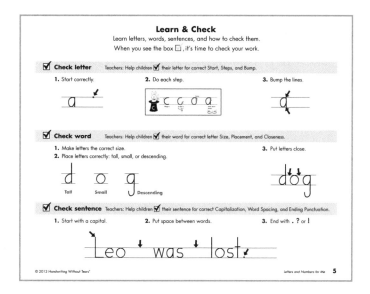

Throughout the workbook you will see opportunities for children to self-check their handwriting. Self-checking helps students understand where they are doing well and where they need improvement. They will put extra effort into making the checked letters and sentences correctly. This also leads to an informal self-checking process in daily writing. When children struggle here, you will know where they need extra attention.

Below is an example of how *Letters and Numbers for Me* is designed to promote self-checking skills. We have highlighted a letter, word, and sentence and the area where your students will self-check.

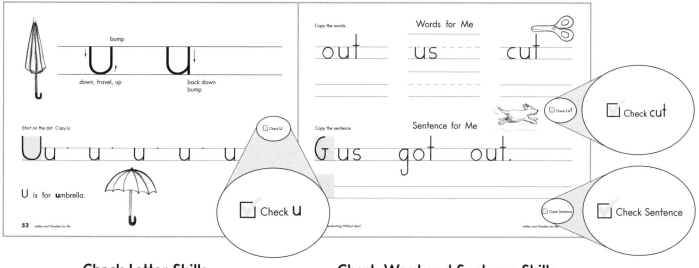

Check Letter Skills   **Check Word and Sentence Skills**

The Hand Activity

The Hand Activity is as much fun as Rock, Paper, Scissors. It's a real-time looking, moving, talking way to teach letter size and place. Children move their hands to show capital or lowercase letters. They move their hands to show tall, small, or descending lowercase letters. This activity is a teacher and child favorite. Note: Avoid using The Hand Activity if there are students in your class who use sign language.

Materials
None

Grouping
Any size

Support/ELL
Use your alphabet wall cards to practice each pair of capital and lowercase letters. Use left hand for capital letters and right hand for lowercase letters.

Left		Right	
A	flat	**a**	fisted
B	flat	**b**	index up
C	flat	**c**	fisted
D	flat	**d**	index up

Activity

Capital & Lowercase Activity - Two Hands
The left (L) hand is the capital. The right (R) hand is the lowercase letter. Show and say the same capital and lowercase letter. Like this:

Capital **C** and lowercase **c**   L hand flat and R hand fisted
Capital **T** and lowercase **t**   L hand flat and R index pointing up
Capital **G** and lowercase **g**   L hand flat and R thumb pointing down

Any Letter Activity - One Hand
This activity shows one letter at a time. Use it to prepare children before they copy words. Spell and show words like this: **dog**.
d - R index pointing up,   **o** - R fisted,   **g** - with R thumb down

✓ Check
Observe children as they move their hands for capital and lowercase.
Do they use their left and right hands correctly for **Cc, Oo, Ss, Vv, Ww**?

More to Learn
Say "tall," "small," and "descending" to describe letter size and place. Use "Descending Letters," track 19, *Rock, Rap, Tap & Learn* CD for **g, j, y, p, q**.

Capital & Lowercase Activity

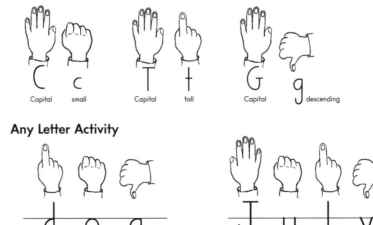

| Capital | small | Capital | tall | Capital | descending |

Any Letter Activity

| tall | small | descending |

CONNECTIONS
▶ **Video Lesson:** View "The Hand Activity" at hwtears.com/videos

Wet-Dry-Try for Lowercase Letters

Blackboards are old-fashioned, but using Wet-Dry-Try on the Blackboard with Double Lines is an innovative teaching strategy. The latest research on brain development supports this activity. This research calls for fewer elements (just two lines), modeling, sensory engagement, and immediate feedback (Sousa 2011).

Materials
- Blackboard with Double Lines* (1 per child)
- Little Chalk Bits (1")
- Little Sponge Cubes (1/2")
- Little cups of water
- Paper towel pieces

Grouping
One-on-one; small group

Support/ELL
This activity supports all children with its individual attention, large size, focused elements, modeling, multisensory appeal, and repetition.

Activity

1. Teacher's Part – Write f with Chalk
Use chalk to write a letter on double lines. Say the step-by-step directions.

2. Child's Part – Wet-Dry-Try
As the child does each part, say the step-by-step directions to guide the child. The child is encouraged to join in, saying the words.
Wet: The child uses a Little Sponge Cube to trace the letter.
Dry: The child uses a little piece of paper towel to trace the letter.
Try: The child uses a Little Chalk Bit to write the letter.

✓ Check
Observe children as they complete the activity. Do they trace the letter correctly? Do they write the letter correctly?

More to Learn
Children will be excited to do this activity with their names and familiar words. Children will write each letter, say it out loud, and then read it.

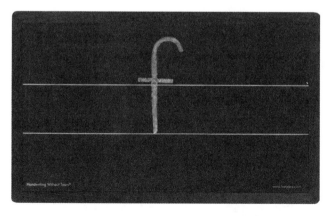

*If you don't have a Blackboard with Double Lines, consider using our Double Line Writer on your whiteboard. This product is available at **hwtears.com**

CONNECTIONS

Language Arts Link: Write letters on the Blackboard with Double Lines and then find things in the room that start with the letter sound.

▶ **Video Lesson:** View "Wet-Dry-Try" at hwtears.com/videos

Letter Stories

Fun stories help children remember letters that are a bit tricky. Beyond our simple verbal cues, we made up some stories that are fun to share and help make these letters memorable.

b

Honeybee
Say, "Let's make letter **h**. Now let's make another **h**. I have a surprise. This is an **h** for a honeybee." Turn **h** into **b**.

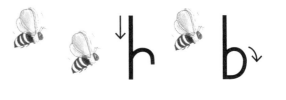

e

Run the Bases
Place the pencil on the dot. Say, "Batter up to bat. Here comes the pitch. Hit the ball, wait, then run the bases: first, second, third, stop! It's not a home run."

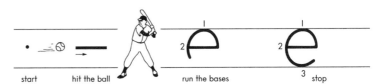

f

Fire Hose Squirts
Say, "**f** is like water squirting out of a fire hose. It goes up and then falls down."

g

If George Falls
Say, "Inside **g** lives a little man named George (draw a little face in **g**). He says, 'Ohhhh, if I fall, will you catch me?' Sure, I will catch you (turn the **g** to catch George) if you fall."

Ohhhh, if I fall, will you catch me?

"Sure, I will catch you if you fall."

k

Karate K
Say, "The Big Line is Mr. Kaye, your karate teacher. He wants you to show him your kick.

K: Put your chalk in the corner. That's you. Now kick Mr. Kaye. Hiiii-ya. That's the karate **K**.

k: Put the pencil on the line. That's you. Now kick Mr. Kaye. Hiiii-ya. That's the karate **k**."

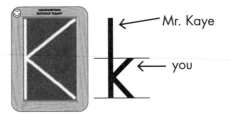

Mr. Kaye

you

m

Stinky m

Say, "If **m** has a big gap, people will throw trash in the gap. Don't make a big gap. Make the gap so little, there is only room for an upside down chocolate kiss."

q

U-Turn

Say, "The letter **q** is followed by **u**.
Think of quiet, quit, quibble, quaint, etc.
At the bottom of **q**, stop and make a U-turn."

s

Stop, Drop & Roll with S

Start **s** with a little **c**. Go over and say hello to the smiley face. Say, "What do you do if your clothes catch on fire? You stop, drop, and roll!"

 Say hello to the smiley face.

 Stop, drop, and roll.

Tt

T Is Tall, t Is Tall But...

Say, "Look at me. I can make capital **T**.
Look at me. I can make lowercase **t**.
Capital **T** is tall.
Lowercase **t** is tall, but it's crossed lower.
Capital **T** and lowercase **t** are both tall."

z

Z Chase

Say, "Left hand says, 'I'm going to chase you.' Right hand picks up the pencil and runs across the page.

Left hand says, 'I'm kidding! Come back.'
Right hand slides back down toward the left hand.

Left hand says, 'Ha! I'm going to chase you.'
Right hand runs back across."

(This story is for right-handers with z reversal problems, but can be adapted for lefties)

Letters, Words & Sentences with Music

As soon as students know nine lowercase letters, you'll teach them how to write sentences! They start with a very simple sentence (I saw a cow.) and the very catchy "Sentence Song." You'll enjoy that song all year long. Look for other songs that will help you teach key letter groups joyfully and well.

Materials
- *Rock, Rap, Tap & Learn* CD, tracks 7, 16, 17, and 19

Grouping
Whole class

Support/ELL
Sing without the CD to slow down the tempo. When you sing or say the words slowly, you can set the tempo and the repeats.

Activity

Track 7: Sentence Song
Children learn to start with a capital, write a word, and leave a space. Sung with the "Yankee Doodle" tune, sentences are such fun.

Track 16: CAPITALS & lowercase
This song teaches capital/lowercase letters: **Cc**, **Oo**, **Ss**, **Vv**, and **Ww**.

Track 17: Magic C Rap
Magic c starts **a**, **d**, and **g**. This song teaches letters with the Magic c.

Track 19: Descending Letters
Singing about **g**, **j**, **y**, **p**, and **q** is fun: **g** and **j** go down and turn, **y** goes sliding down, **p** goes straight down, and **q** goes down with a U-turn.

✓ Check
Observe children as they listen to these songs. Are they singing? Do they use movements? Do they understand the concepts?

More to Learn
Use "Vowels," track 11, to teach **a**, **e**, **i**, **o**, and **u** as a group. The names of the letters are long vowels. Now teach children the short vowel sounds.

CONNECTIONS

🔘 **Technology Link:** Use the Digital Teaching Tools to look at the letters and reinforce alphabet knowledge as you sing. Visit **hwtears.com/dtt**

Diver Letters' School

This fun song for the Diver Letters (**p**, **r**, **n**, **m**, **h**, and **b**) will have your students moving! Both you and children will love this activity. Make sure to swim to your left so that your students will swim over the right way! When you do **h** and **b**, pretend it's a high dive. "Climb" up the ladder to the high diving board.

Materials
• *Rock, Rap, Tap & Learn* CD, "Diver Letters' School," track 18

Grouping
Whole class

Support/ELL
After demonstrating the diver motion, finger trace or write a larger model of **p**, **r**, **n**, **m**, **h**, and **b**, while saying the directions (diver motions) out loud.

Activity
1. Write letters **p**, **r**, **n**, **m**, **h**, and **b** on the board.

2. Point to the letters. Explain that **p**, **r**, **n**, **m**, **h**, and **b** all start with a diving motion: dive down, swim up, and over (demonstrate).

3. Play "Diver Letters' School."

4. Children imitate the motions as they sing.

Note: Toss out imaginary swimming suits for your class to put on. Bring in your own whistle to whistle with the CD.

✓ Check
Check to make sure students are imitating the diver motions correctly. Can they say the motions out loud while they correctly form a Diver Letter?

More to Learn
Walk around the room and look for words that start with Diver Letters. Make a list of words on a large easel or board.

CONNECTIONS

Social Studies Link: Talk about diving. Discuss the Olympics. Bring in pictures of other sports that happen at the Olympics. Discuss children's favorite sports.

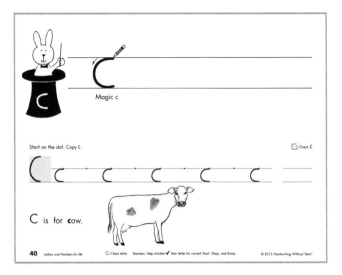

Magic c

Start on the dot. Copy C.

Check C

C is for cow.

40 Letters and Numbers for Me   ☐ Check letter.   Teachers: Help children ✔ their letter for correct Start, Steps, and Bump.   © 2013 Handwriting Without Tears®

OBJECTIVE: To write lowercase **c** with correct formation.

Lesson Plan
Let's find the lowercase c page. Help children turn to p. 40. Discuss what's on the page.

1. Demonstrate
Demonstrate **c** on the Blackboard with Double Lines, whiteboard, or flip chart.
Use "CAPITALS & lowercase," track 16, *Rock, Rap, Tap, & Learn* CD.
Children finger trace the large lowercase **c** model in their workbooks.

2. Copy
Prepare for writing with good posture, pencil grip, and use of the helper hand.
Demonstrate **c** again, saying, "Magic c" together.
Children watch, then copy **c**'s.

3. Check & Evaluate
Help children ☑ their letter for correct Start, Steps, and Bump.
Evaluate the correct formation for lowercase **c**.

Read, Color & Draw
Read the sentence together. Point out the beginning of capital **C** and the lowercase **c** in cow.
Encourage free coloring and drawing. Add grass, a sun, etc.

More to Learn
Introduce sentence writing skills, using "**C** is for **c**ow."
1. Capitalize the first word. 2. Add space between words.
3. End with a period.

Support/ELL
Preview **c** with Wet-Dry-Try on the Blackboard with Double Lines (p. 105). In the workbook, write each **c** with a highlighter for child to pencil trace.

CONNECTIONS

Math Link: Count tail, ears, legs, and spots on the cow.
Look at pictures of other animals. What can you count on them?

O

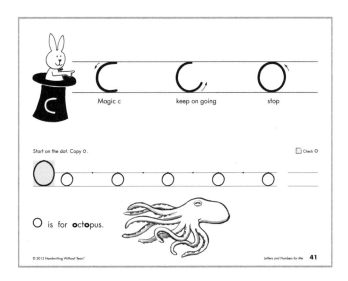

OBJECTIVE: To write lowercase **o** with correct formation.

Lesson Plan
Let's find the lowercase o page. Help children turn to p. 41. Discuss what's on the page.

1. Demonstrate
Demonstrate on the Blackboard with Double Lines, whiteboard, or flip chart.
Use The Hand Activity for **O** and **o** (multisensory activity p. 104).
Children finger trace the large lowercase **o** model in their workbooks.

2. Copy
Prepare for writing with good posture, pencil grip, and use of the helper hand.
Demonstrate **o** again, saying the step-by-step directions together.
Children watch, then copy **o**'s.

3. Check & Evaluate
Help children ☑ their letter for correct Start, Steps, and Bump.
Evaluate the correct formation for lowercase **o**.

Read, Color & Draw
Read the sentence together. Point out the beginning of capital **O** and the lowercase **o**'s in octopus.
Encourage free coloring and drawing. Add water, fish, etc.

More to Learn
The symbol **O** works as a letter, a shape (circle) and a number (zero). All of them begin with Magic c.

Support/ELL
Slowly repeat the step-by-step directions, exactly as they appear. Help left-handed children begin **o** with Magic c. Left-handed children are more likely to begin letter **o** incorrectly.

CONNECTIONS

Math Link: Count the tentacles on the octopus. Count legs on stuffed animals. Allow children to bring in their own animals from home for this fun counting activity.

little Magic c   + turn down   + curve around

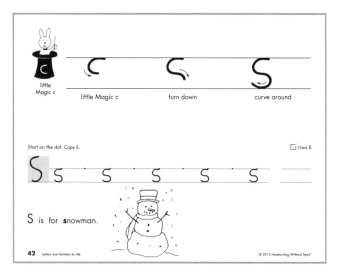

little Magic c   turn down   curve around

Start on the dot. Copy s.   ☐ Check S

S is for **s**nowman.

42   *Letters and Numbers for Me*   © 2013 Handwriting Without Tears®

OBJECTIVE: To write lowercase **s** with correct formation.

Lesson Plan
Let's find the lowercase s page. Help children turn to p. 42. Discuss what's on the page.

1. **Demonstrate**
   Demonstrate **s** on the Blackboard with Double Lines, whiteboard, or flip chart.
   Use Letter Story for **s** (multisensory activity p. 107).
   Children finger trace the large lowercase **s** model in their workbooks.

2. **Copy**
   Prepare for writing with good posture, pencil grip, and use of the helper hand.
   Demonstrate **s** again, saying the step-by-step directions together.
   Children watch, then copy **s**'s.

3. **Check & Evaluate**
   Help children ☑ their letter for correct Start, Steps, and Bump.
   Evaluate the correct formation for lowercase **s**.

Read, Color & Draw
Read the sentence together. Point out the beginning of capital **S** and the lowercase **s** in snowman.
Encourage free coloring and drawing. Add snowflakes, another snowman, etc.

More to Learn
Teach sentence writing skills, using "**S** is for **s**nowman."
1. Capitalize the first word. 2. Add space between words.
3. End with a period.

Support/ELL
Use dough to make a snake and then turn the snake
into **S**. Teach left-handed students to copy from the model
on the right.

CONNECTIONS

Social Studies Link: Discuss places in the world where
it snows. Place small, cut-out snowmen on the map
where you can build snowmen.

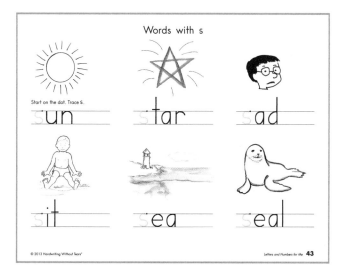

OBJECTIVE: To practice writing lowercase **s**.

Lesson Plan

Help children turn to p. 43. Read the title. Then, read the words together.

1. **Read and spell the first word, sun.**
   Have children point to the picture of the sun.
   Read the word sun together.
   Slowly spell the word sun together: **s - u - n**.

2. **Trace s in sun.**
   Prepare for writing with good posture, pencil grip, and use of the helper hand.
   Tell children to start on the dot and trace **s**.

3. **Continue with each word.**
   Repeat with star, sad, sit, sea, and seal.
   Read and spell each word together. Then write **s**, starting on the dot.
   Evaluate children as they write letters.

Color & Draw

Encourage free coloring and drawing. Remind children to add details.

More to Learn

Use The Hand Activity (p. 104) to preview tall and small letters. Small letters fit in the middle space. Tall letters use the top space.

Support/ELL

For children who have difficulty writing lowercase **s**, demonstrate on the Blackboard with Double Lines (p. 105). Allow child to finger trace your model.

CONNECTIONS

Language Arts Link: Point out the word "sad." Discuss feelings. Provide children with a prompt to complete: "I am sad when..." or "When I am sad..."

slide down + slide up

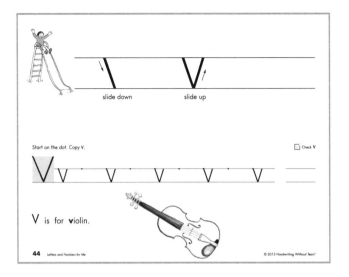

Start on the dot. Copy V.

☐ Check V

V is for **v**iolin.

44 *Letters and Numbers for Me*   © 2013 Handwriting Without Tears®

OBJECTIVE: To write lowercase **v** with correct formation.

Lesson Plan
Let's find the lowercase v page. Help children turn to p. 44. Discuss what's on the page.

1. Demonstrate
Demonstrate **v** on the Blackboard with Double Lines, whiteboard, or flip chart.
Use "Sliding Down to the End of the Alphabet," track 15, *Rock, Rap, Tap & Learn* CD.
Children finger trace the large lowercase **v** model in their workbooks.

2. Copy
Prepare for writing with good posture, pencil grip, and use of the helper hand.
Demonstrate **v** again, saying the step-by-step directions together.
Children watch, then copy **v**'s.

3. Check & Evaluate
Help children ☑ their letter for correct Start, Steps, and Bump.
Evaluate the correct formation for lowercase **v**.

Read, Color & Draw
Read the sentence together. Point out the beginning of capital **V** and the lowercase **v** in violin.
Encourage free coloring and drawing. Show children how to draw music notes.

More to Learn
Teach sentence writing skills, using "**V** is for **v**iolin."
1. Capitalize the first word. 2. Add space between words.
3. End with a period.

Support/ELL
Use Wood Pieces to make **V**'s (p. 38). Review words:
top, bottom, and open.

CONNECTIONS

Language Arts Link: Listen to classical music. Talk
about the different instruments that you may be hearing:
the violin, the cello, the viola, the piano, etc.

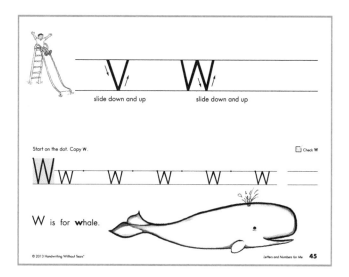

OBJECTIVE: To write lowercase **w** with correct formation.

Lesson Plan
Let's find the lowercase w page. Help children turn to p. 45. Discuss what's on the page.

1. **Demonstrate**
   Demonstrate **w** on the Blackboard with Double Lines, whiteboard, or flip chart.
   Use "Sliding Down to the End of the Alphabet," track 15, *Rock, Rap, Tap & Learn* CD.
   Children finger trace the large lowercase **w** model in their workbooks.

2. **Copy**
   Prepare for writing with good posture, pencil grip, and use of the helper hand.
   Demonstrate **w** again, saying the step-by-step directions together.
   Children watch, then copy **w**'s.

3. **Check & Evaluate**
   Help children ☑ their letter for correct Start, Steps, and Bump.
   Evaluate the correct formation for lowercase **w**.

Read, Color & Draw
Read the sentence together. Point out the beginning of capital **W** and the lowercase **w** in whale.
Encourage free coloring and drawing. Add water, small fish, etc.

More to Learn
Review capital and lowercase **Cc, Oo, Ss, Vv,** and **Ww**
with The Hand Activity (p. 104).

Support/ELL
Two children use their Wood Piece **V**'s to make one **W**
(p. 38). This is a fun, cooperative activity for pairs.
Review words: apart and together.

CONNECTIONS

Science Link: Find videos of different whales to watch.
Discuss their look, size, sounds, etc. Discuss other
animals in the ocean. Locate oceans on a map.

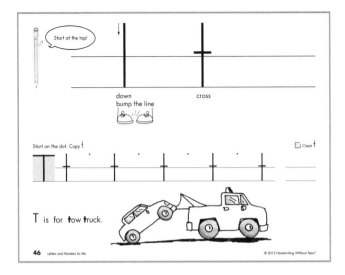

OBJECTIVE: To write lowercase **t** with correct formation.

Lesson Plan
Let's find the lowercase t page. Help children turn to p. 46. Discuss what's on the page.

1. Demonstrate
Demonstrate **t** on the Blackboard with Double Lines, whiteboard, or flip chart.
Use Letter Story for **T** and **t** (multisensory activity p. 107).
Children finger trace the large lowercase **t** model in their workbooks.

2. Copy
Prepare for writing with good posture, pencil grip, and use of the helper hand.
Demonstrate **t** again, saying the step-by-step directions together.
Children watch, then copy **t**'s.

3. Check & Evaluate
Help children ☑ their letter for correct Start, Steps, and Bump.
Evaluate the correct formation for lowercase **t**.

Read, Color & Draw
Read the sentence together. Point out the beginning of capital **T** and the lowercase **t**'s in tow truck.
Encourage free coloring and drawing. Add a road, dirt, etc.

More to Learn
Teach sentence writing skills using "T is for tow truck."
1. Capitalize the first word. 2. Add space between words.
3. End with a period.

Support/ELL
Help left-handed children with crossing **T** or **t**. It is natural and easier for them to pull from right to left. Draw an arrow on the model as a reminder.

CONNECTIONS

Language Arts Link: Use a Venn diagram to compare a truck to a car. Read stories about transportation.
Find capital **T** and lowercase **t** in the books.

Copy the words.   Words for Me

to   two   cow

cot   tot   so

☐ Check so

© 2013 Handwriting Without Tears®   ☐ Check word.   Teachers: Help children ✓ their word for correct letter Size, Placement, and Closeness.   *Letters and Numbers for Me*   **47**

OBJECTIVE: To practice writing words correctly on different lines.

Lesson Plan
Help children turn to p. 47. Read the words together. Look for lowercase **t** in each word.

1. Demonstrate words for children to copy.
Prepare double lines for **to**, triple lines for **two**, and double lines for **cow**.
Demonstrate **to**, **two**, and **cow**. Children copy all the words.

2. Demonstrate more words for children to copy.
Prepare double lines for **cot**, triple lines for **tot**, and double lines for **so**.
Demonstrate **cot**, **tot**, and **so**. Children copy all words.

3. Check & Evaluate
Help children ☑ their word for correct Size, Placement, and Closeness.
Evaluate children as they copy the words and help them as needed.

Read, Color & Draw
Read the words together.
Encourage free coloring, perhaps a border on the page or around the title.

More to Learn
This is the first page of the workbook where you ☑ the word. Review Size, Placement, and Closeness with children. See p. 5 in the workbook.

Support/ELL
Explain the names of lines. "Double lines have two lines, a base line and a mid line. Triple lines have three lines, a base line, a mid line with dashes, and a top line."

CONNECTIONS

Language Arts Link: When discussing lines, teach positions top, middle, and bottom. Use objects and point to top, middle, and bottom.

🏠 **Home Link:** This is the end of the first letter group **c, o, s, v, w,** and **t**. A description of these letters and home practice is available at **hwtears.com/click**

Voices

Children should learn to write letters in the correct sequence. If you demonstrate with different voices, your students will quickly learn and memorize all the steps. This activity is filled with the repetition children need, but it is so much fun that the repetition is never boring.

Materials
- Large board, prepared with double lines
- Magic C Bunny Puppet

Grouping
Any size

Support/ELL
Talk about inside voices and outside voices. Let the Magic C Bunny ask children for other voice suggestions: spooky, shaky, robotic, operatic, etc.

Activity

1. Help children find the step-by-step words in their workbooks. Read the words together as children point. Demonstrate the letter, saying the steps with the children.

2. Let the Magic C Bunny whisper a request for a different voice. Slowly demonstrate the letter again using a new voice. Children join in by saying the steps and modeling your voice. Repeat.

3. Write the letter. Children put their pencils on the dot. They use their voices together to say the steps as they write.

4. Repeat the activity with different voices: high, low, loud, soft, slow, fast.

✓ Check
Observe students during the activity. Do they point to the steps and "read" the words correctly? Can they repeat the directions?

More to Learn
Teach new vocabulary like "silly," "deep," and "high." Explain that words like "high" or "deep" can have different meanings.

CONNECTIONS

▶ **Video Lesson:** View "Teaching with Voices" at hwtears.com/videos

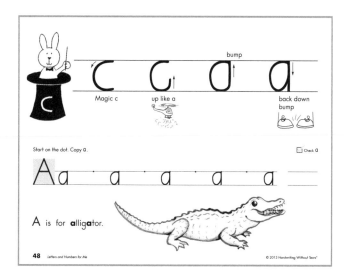

OBJECTIVE: To write lowercase **a** with correct formation.

Lesson Plan
Let's find the lowercase a page. Help children turn to p. 48. Discuss what's on the page.

1. **Demonstrate**
   Demonstrate **a** on the Blackboard with Double Lines, whiteboard, or flip chart.
   Use Voices for **a** (multisensory activity p. 118).
   Children finger trace the large lowercase **a** model in their workbooks.

2. **Copy**
   Prepare for writing with good posture, pencil grip, and use of the helper hand.
   Demonstrate **a** again, saying the step-by-step directions together with voices.
   Children watch, then copy **a**'s.

3. **Check & Evaluate**
   Help children ☑ their letter for correct Start, Steps, and Bump.
   Evaluate the correct formation for lowercase **a**.

Read, Color & Draw
Read the sentence together. Point out the beginning of capital **A** and the lowercase **a**'s in alligator.
Encourage free coloring and drawing. Add rocks, grass, water, etc.

More to Learn
Explain that some lowercase letters look like their capitals but others don't. Look at **Aa**, **Dd**, and **Gg**.

Support/ELL
If **a** is too skinny, start on the dot and travel on the line before curving down. Review **a** with large movements used during Air Writing.

CONNECTIONS

Social Studies Link: Discuss alligators. Louisiana is the state with the largest alligator population. Florida and Louisiana have more than one million alligators each!

d Magic c + up like a helicopter + up higher + back down, bump

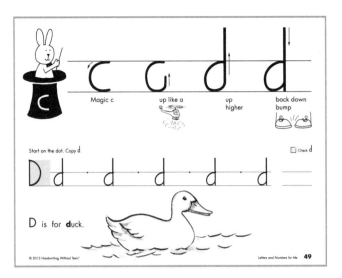

Magic c   up like a   up   back down
                 helicopter   higher   bump

Start on the dot. Copy d.   ☐ Check d

D d   d   d   d   d

D is for **d**uck.

© 2013 Handwriting Without Tears®   Letters and Numbers for Me **49**

OBJECTIVE: To write lowercase **d** with correct formation.

Lesson Plan
Let's find the lowercase d page. Help children turn to p. 49. Discuss what's on the page.

1. Demonstrate
Demonstrate **d** on the Blackboard with Double Lines, whiteboard, or flip chart.
Use Voices for **d** (multisensory activity p. 118).
Children finger trace the large lowercase **d** model in their workbooks.

2. Copy
Prepare for writing with good posture, pencil grip, and use of the helper hand.
Demonstrate **d** again, saying the step-by-step directions together.
Children watch, then copy **d**'s.

3. Check & Evaluate
Help children ☑ their letter for correct Start, Steps, and Bump.
Evaluate the correct formation for lowercase **d**.

Read, Color & Draw
Read the sentence together. Point out the beginning of capital **D** and the lowercase **d** in duck.
Encourage free coloring and drawing. Add water, grass, flowers, etc.

More to Learn
Go on a scavenger hunt inside the classroom or outside
to look for letter **d**.

Support/ELL
Teach an alphabet rhyme to remember how to make **d**.
Say, "**a**, **b**, **c**. Magic c turns into **d**." Demonstrate as you
repeat the rhyme.

CONNECTIONS

Language Arts Link: Talk about words with different
meanings. A duck is a bird. The word duck also means
to bend suddenly.

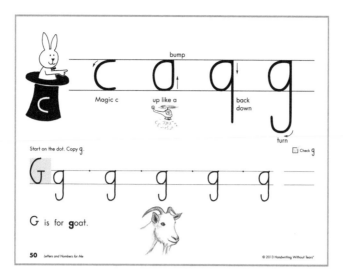

OBJECTIVE: To write lowercase **g** with correct formation.

Lesson Plan
Let's find the lowercase g page. Help children turn to p. 50. Discuss what's on the page.

1. Demonstrate
Demonstrate **g** on the Blackboard with Double Lines, whiteboard, or flip chart.
Use Letter Story for **g** (multisensory activity p. 106).
Children finger trace the large lowercase **g** model in their workbooks.

2. Copy
Prepare for writing with good posture, pencil grip, and use of the helper hand.
Demonstrate **g** again, saying the step-by-step directions together.
Children watch, then copy **g**'s.

3. Check & Evaluate
Help children ☑ their letter for correct Start, Steps, and Bump.
Evaluate the correct formation for lowercase **g**.

Read, Color & Draw
Read the sentence together. Point out the beginning of capital **G** and the lowercase **g** in goat.
Encourage free coloring and drawing. Add grass, sun, etc.

More to Learn
Make a matching game for capitals and lowercase letters they have already learned. Have children work in pairs to match the letters.

Support/ELL
Preview **g** with Wet-Dry-Try on the Blackboard with Double Lines (p. 105). In the workbook, highlight **g**'s for child to pencil trace.

CONNECTIONS

Science Link: Compare and contrast cows and goats. How are they alike? How are they different? Do goats make milk?

🏠 **Home Link:** This is the end of the Magic c Letters Group **a**, **d**, and **g**. A description of these letters and home practice is available at **hwtears.com/click**

Sentence Song

Why do some children runwordstogether? Speech doesn't use spaces between words. Children may naturally write like they talk, without spaces. Bad worksheets can also force children to squeeze words together. By teaching with "Sentence Song" and generous spaces, you boost sentence skills.

Materials
- *Rock, Rap, Tap & Learn* CD, "Sentence Song," track 7

Grouping
Whole class

Support/ELL
Images help children understand the sentences. Use color tiles for a visual of how many words are in the sentence.

Activity

1. Teach sentence skills as you write: "We can write." on double lines.

2. Teach each sentence part as you write:
   W = I start the sentence with a capital letter.
   We = I write a word and leave a space. (Be generous!)
   We can = I write a word and leave a space.
   We can write. = I write the last word. This is the end. I make a period.

3. Play "Sentence Song." Play it again and sing along while you point to the capitalization, spacing, and punctuation with your students.

✓ Check
Observe children as you write and explain all the parts of a sentence. Do they know the words to the song? Do they point correctly?

More to Learn
Sentence School® has lesson plans and word cards for a wonderful year of action, describing, and asking sentences (p. 189).

CONNECTIONS

Language Arts Link: Clap out the number of syllables in words. This also links the activity to beginning kindergarten reading skills.

Copy the sentences.

Sentences for Me

I saw a cow.

I saw a goat.

☐ Check Sentences

© 2013 Handwriting Without Tears®   ☐ Check sentence.   Teachers: Help children ✓ their sentence for correct Capitalization, Word Spacing, and Ending Punctuation.   *Letters and Numbers for Me*   **51**

OBJECTIVE: To write sentences correctly.

Lesson Plan

Help children turn to p. 51. Read the two sentences together.

1. **Demonstrate the first two words for children to copy.**
   Prepare double lines.
   Use "Sentence Song," track 7, *Rock, Rap, Tap & Learn* CD.
   Demonstrate **I saw**. Explain capital, space, word. Children copy.

2. **Demonstrate the rest of the sentence for children to copy.**
   Demonstrate **a cow**. Explain word, space, word.
   Demonstrate adding a period to end the sentence. Children copy.
   Have children copy the next sentence.

3. **Check & Evaluate**
   Help children ☑ their sentence for correct Capitalization, Word Spacing, and Ending Punctuation.
   Evaluate children as they copy the sentences, and help them as needed.

Read, Color & Draw

Read the words and sentences together.
Encourage free coloring and drawing.

More to Learn

This is the first page of the workbook where we do ☑ the sentence. Review Capitalization, Word Spacing, and Ending Punctuation with children. See p. 5 in their workbook.

Support/ELL

Always use at least two fingers spacing when you write sentences for children to copy.

CONNECTIONS

Language Arts Link: Look through favorite books and have children locate sentences. How do they know it is a sentence?

---

u

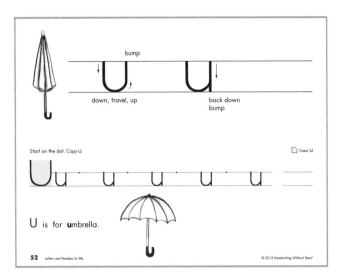

OBJECTIVE: To write lowercase **u** with correct formation.

Lesson Plan
Let's find the lowercase u page. Help children turn to p. 52. Discuss what's on the page.

1. Demonstrate
Demonstrate **u** on the Blackboard with Double Lines, whiteboard, or flip chart.
Use "Vowels," track 11, *Rock, Rap, Tap & Learn* CD.
Children finger trace the large lowercase **u** model in their workbooks.

2. Copy
Prepare for writing with good posture, pencil grip, and use of the helper hand.
Demonstrate **u** again, saying the step-by-step directions together.
Children watch, then copy **u**'s.

3. Check & Evaluate
Help children ☑ their letter for correct Start, Steps, and Bump.
Evaluate the correct formation for lowercase **u**.

Read, Color & Draw
Read the sentence together. Point out the beginning of capital **U**, and the lowercase **u** in umbrella.
Encourage free coloring and drawing. Add rain drops, a cloud, etc.

More to Learn
Help children find the subtle difference between capital **U** and lowercase **u**. Encourage children to travel on the bottom line before going up if **u** is too pointed.

Support/ELL
Take time to reread the lowercase letter pages together starting with p. 40 in the workbook. Read just the lowercase letters **c**, **o**, **s**, **v**, **w**, **t**, **a**, **d**, and **g**.

CONNECTIONS

Science Link: Discuss rain. Why does it rain? What do we have to do when it rains? Discuss the water cycle.

Words & Sentence for Me

OBJECTIVE: To practice writing words and a sentence correctly.

Lesson Plan
Help children turn to p. 53. Read the words and sentence together.

1. **Demonstrate the words for children to copy.**
   Prepare double lines for **out**, triple lines for **us**, and double lines for **cut**.
   Demonstrate **out**, **us**, and **cut**. Children copy all words.

2. **Demonstrate the sentence for children to copy.**
   Prepare double lines.
   Use "Sentence Song," track 7, *Rock, Rap, Tap & Learn* CD.
   Demonstrate **Gus got out.** for children to copy.

3. **Check & Evaluate**
   Help children ☑ their word for correct Size, Placement, and Closeness.
   Help children ☑ their sentence for correct Capitalization, Word Spacing, and Ending Punctuation.
   Evaluate children as they copy the words and sentences, and help them as needed.

Read, Color & Draw
Read the words and sentence together.
Encourage free coloring and drawing.

More to Learn
Children build writing fluency by practicing new letters with familiar ones. Help children look for lowercase **u** in words around the room or in books.

Support/ELL
Support good sentence spacing by showing children how to use two fingers to add space between words.

CONNECTIONS

⏻ **Technology Link:** Write sentences together as a class. Use the A+ Worksheet Maker to make practice sentences. Visit **hwtears.com/dtt**

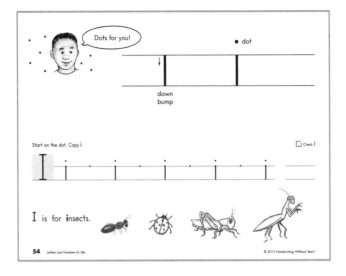

OBJECTIVE: To write lowercase **i** with correct formation.

Lesson Plan

Let's find the lowercase i page. Help children turn to p. 54. Discuss what's on the page.

1. Demonstrate

Demonstrate **i** on the Blackboard with Double Lines, whiteboard, or flip chart.
Use "Vowels," track 11, *Rock, Rap, Tap & Learn* CD.
Children finger trace the large lowercase **i** model in their workbooks.

2. Copy

Prepare for writing with good posture, pencil grip, and use of the helper hand.
Demonstrate **i** again, saying the step-by-step directions together.
Children watch, then copy **i**'s.

3. Check & Evaluate

Help children ☑ their letter for correct Start, Steps, and Bump.
Evaluate the correct formation for lowercase **i**.

Read, Color & Draw

Read the sentence together. Point out the beginning of capital **I** and the lowercase **i** in insects.
Encourage free coloring and drawing. Add grass, more insects, etc.

More to Learn

The boy at the top has a quote bubble. Bring in a newspaper with a comic strip to show children. Explain that quotations are the exact words out of a person's mouth.

Support/ELL

Before you discuss the page, teach children the names of the insects on the page: ant, ladybug, grasshopper, and praying mantis.

CONNECTIONS

Science Link: Discuss insects. How many legs do they have? How are they different? How are they alike?

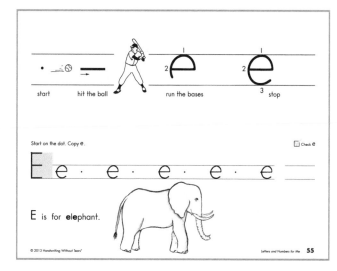

start   + hit the ball   + run the bases   + stop

e

OBJECTIVE: To write lowercase **e** with correct formation.

Lesson Plan

Let's find the lowercase e page. Help children turn to p. 55. Discuss what's on the page.

1. Demonstrate

Demonstrate **e** on the Blackboard with Double Lines, whiteboard, or flip chart.
Use Letter Story for **e** (multisensory activity p. 106).
Children finger trace the large lowercase **e** model in their workbooks.

2. Copy

Prepare for writing with good posture, pencil grip, and use of the helper hand.
Demonstrate **e** again, saying the step-by-step directions together.
Children watch, then copy **e**'s.

3. Check & Evaluate

Help children ☑ their letter for correct Start, Steps, and Bump.
Evaluate the correct formation for lowercase **e**.

Read, Color & Draw

Read the sentence together. Point out the beginning of capital **E** and the lowercase **e**'s in elephant.
Encourage free coloring and drawing. Add peanuts, water, etc.

More to Learn

All of the vowels have been taught. Vowels are the glue that hold words together! Use "Vowels," track 11, *Rock, Rap, Tap & Learn* CD to review **a**, **e**, **i**, **o**, and **u**.

Support/ELL

Preview **e** with Wet-Dry-Try on the Blackboard with Double Lines (p. 105). In the workbook, write each **e** with a highlighter for child to pencil trace.

CONNECTIONS

Language Arts Link: Read a story book about elephants. Discuss the characters and events in the story.

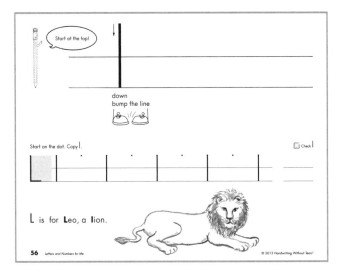

OBJECTIVE: To write lowercase l with correct formation.

Lesson Plan
Let's find the lowercase l page. Help children turn to p. 56. Discuss what's on the page.

1. Demonstrate
Demonstrate l on the Blackboard with Double Lines, whiteboard, or flip chart.
Use Air Writing for l (multisensory activity p. 61).
Children finger trace the large lowercase l model in their workbooks.

2. Copy
Prepare for writing with good posture, pencil grip, and use of the helper hand.
Demonstrate l again, saying the step-by-step directions together.
Children watch, then copy l's.

3. Check & Evaluate
Help children ☑ their letter for correct Start, Steps, and Bump.
Evaluate the correct formation for lowercase l.

Read, Color & Draw
Read the sentence together. Point out the beginning of capital **L**, the capital **L** in Leo, and lowercase l in lion. Encourage free coloring and drawing. Add trees, grass, etc.

More to Learn
Capital letters begin proper nouns. Your students are ready to learn the difference between Leo and lion. Leo, like their names, begins with a capital.

Support/ELL
Take time to reread the lowercase letter pages together starting with p. 40 in their workbooks. Read just the lowercase letters: **c, o, s, v, w, t, a, d, g, u, i, e,** and now **l**.

CONNECTIONS

Language Arts Link: Place emphasis on the /l/ sound. Extend the sentence, "Leo is a long lazy lion that likes licorice and is lost." Have children add more l words.

Science Link: Discuss constellations. Show children the constellation of Leo. Show a picture of the constellation and how it looks like a lion.

Words & Sentence for Me

Copy the words. Words for Me
dig   will   gate

☐ Check gate

Copy the sentence. Sentence for Me
Leo   was   lost.

☐ Check Sentence

© 2013 Handwriting Without Tears® Letters and Numbers for Me **57**

OBJECTIVE: To practice writing words and a sentence correctly.

Lesson Plan
Help children turn to p. 57. Read the words and sentence together.

1. **Demonstrate the words for children to copy.**
   Prepare double lines for **dig**, triple lines for **will**, and double lines for **gate**.
   Demonstrate **dig**, **will**, and **gate**. Children copy all words.

2. **Demonstrate the sentence for children to copy.**
   Prepare double lines.
   Use "Sentence Song," track 7, *Rock, Rap, Tap & Learn* CD.
   Demonstrate **Leo was lost.** for children to copy.

3. **Check & Evaluate**
   Help children ☑ their word for correct Size, Placement, and Closeness.
   Help children ☑ their sentence for correct Capitalization, Word Spacing, and Ending Punctuation.
   Evaluate children as they copy the words and sentences, and help them as needed.

Read, Color & Draw
Read the words and sentence together.
Encourage free coloring and drawing.

More to Learn
Use The Hand Activity (p. 104) to develop awareness
of tall, small, and descending letters.

Support/ELL
Encourage children to repeat the sentences as they
write them. Help them create their own simple sentences
for illustrations.

CONNECTIONS

Language Arts Link: Model different sentences.
Discuss how to begin with a capital and end with
a punctuation mark.

k

down, bump the line   + kick!   + slide away

OBJECTIVE: To write lowercase **k** with correct formation.

Lesson Plan
Let's find the lowercase k page. Help children turn to p. 58. Discuss what's on the page.

1. Demonstrate
Demonstrate **k** on the Blackboard with Double Lines, whiteboard, or flip chart.
Use Letter Story for **k** (multisensory activity p. 106).
Children finger trace the large lowercase **k** model in their workbooks.

2. Copy
Prepare for writing with good posture, pencil grip, and use of the helper hand.
Demonstrate **k** again, saying the step-by-step directions together.
Children watch, then copy **k**'s.

3. Check & Evaluate
Help children ☑ their letter for correct Start, Steps, and Bump.
Evaluate the correct formation for lowercase **k**.

Read, Color & Draw
Read the sentence together. Point out the beginning of capital **K** and the lowercase **k** in kangaroos.
Encourage free coloring and drawing. Add grass, flowers, sun, etc.

More to Learn
Use Air Writing for **k** (p. 61). When facing children, make the letter backwards for you (start on your right), so it will be correct for them.

Support/ELL
Many young (self-taught) writers form **K** and **k** inefficiently. They make the kick by starting on the Big Line and using two separate strokes. Carefully teach a continuous kick stroke.

CONNECTIONS

Language Arts Link: Write a class story about a kangaroo. Write the story on an easel. Circle all the **k**'s in the story.

Words & Sentence for Me

OBJECTIVE: To practice writing words and a sentence correctly.

Lesson Plan
Help children turn to p. 59. Read the words and sentence together.

1. **Demonstrate the words for children to copy.**
   Prepare double lines for **kit**, triple lines for **doll**, and double lines for **cake**.
   Demonstrate **kit**, **doll**, and **cake**. Children copy all words.

2. **Demonstrate the sentence for children to copy.**
   Prepare double lines.
   Demonstrate **We like kites.** for children to copy.

3. **Check & Evaluate**
   Help children ☑ their word for correct Size, Placement, and Closeness.
   Help children ☑ their sentence for correct Capitalization, Word Spacing, and Ending Punctuation.
   Evaluate children as they copy the words and sentence, and help them as needed.

Read, Color & Draw
Read the words and sentence together.
Encourage free coloring and drawing. Add more kites, clouds, sun, etc.

More to Learn
You can easily help children draw kites. Show them how to write a large lowercase **t** and turn it into a kite. It's even more fun to make tilted **t**'s, so the kites fly away.

Support/ELL
Help children clap the number of words in the sentence.
Point to the capital, spaces between words, and the period.

CONNECTIONS

⏻ **Technology Link:** Write sentences together as a class. Use the A+ Worksheet Maker to make practice sentences. Visit **hwtears.com/dtt**

y

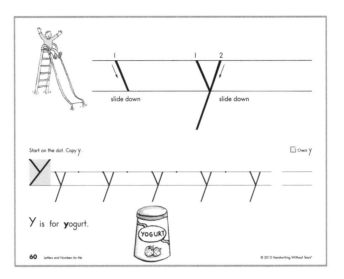

OBJECTIVE: To write lowercase **y** with correct formation.

Lesson Plan
Let's find the lowercase y page. Help children turn to p. 60. Discuss what's on the page.

1. Demonstrate
Demonstrate **y** on the Blackboard with Double Lines, whiteboard, or flip chart.
Use "Sliding Down to the End of the Alphabet," track 15, *Rock, Rap, Tap & Learn* CD.
Children finger trace the large lowercase **y** model in their workbooks.

2. Copy
Prepare for writing with good posture, pencil grip, and use of the helper hand.
Demonstrate **y** again, saying the step-by-step directions together.
Children watch, then copy **y**'s.

3. Check & Evaluate
Help children ☑ their letter for correct Start, Steps, and Bump.
Evaluate the correct formation for lowercase **y**.

Read, Color & Draw
Read the sentence together. Point out the beginning of capital **Y** and the lowercase **y** in yogurt.
Encourage free coloring and drawing. Add other foods, a spoon, etc.

More to Learn
Use "Descending Letters," track 19, *Rock, Rap, Tap & Learn*
CD for **g**, **j**, **y**, **p**, and **q**.

Support/ELL
Use Wet-Dry-Try for **y** on the Blackboard with Double Lines
(p. 105).

CONNECTIONS

Science Link: Bring in yogurt and allow children to use
their senses. What does it look, smell, feel, and taste
like? Compare to something salty and textured.

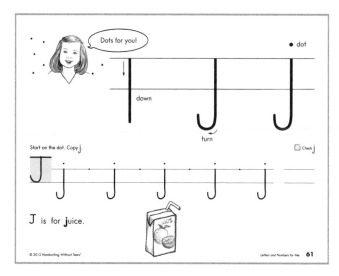

OBJECTIVE: To write lowercase **j** with correct formation.

Lesson Plan
Let's find the lowercase j page. Help children turn to p. 61. Discuss what's on the page.

1. Demonstrate
Demonstrate **j** on the Blackboard with Double Lines, whiteboard, or flip chart.
Use "Descending Letters," track 19, *Rock, Rap, Tap & Learn* CD.
Children finger trace the large lowercase **j** model in their workbooks.

2. Copy
Prepare for writing with good posture, pencil grip, and use of the helper hand.
Demonstrate **j** again, saying the step-by-step directions together.
Children watch, then copy **j**'s.

3. Check & Evaluate
Help children ☑ their letter for correct Start, Steps, and Bump.
Evaluate the correct formation for lowercase **j**.

Read, Color & Draw
Read the sentence together. Point out the beginning of capital **J** and the lowercase **j** in juice.
Encourage free coloring and drawing. Add fruit, a plate, etc.

More to Learn
Use "Descending Letters," track 19, *Rock, Rap, Tap & Learn* CD for **g**, **j**, **y**, **p**, and **q**.

Support/ELL
Lowercase **j** is a low frequency letter. Children are likely to forget its name and how to make it. Point out **j** in the words jump and just.

CONNECTIONS

Math Link: Take a class vote. Do children like apple juice or orange juice? Make a chart and count the number of children for each.

🏠 **Home Link:** This is the end of the Transition Group **u**, **i**, **e**, **l**, **k**, **y**, and **j**. A description of these letters and home practice is available at **hwtears.com/click**

dive down   + swim up and over   + around, bump

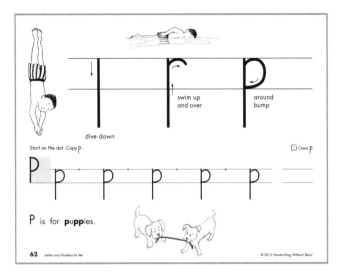

OBJECTIVE: To write lowercase **p** with correct formation.

Lesson Plan
Let's find the lowercase p page. Help children turn to p. 62. Discuss what's on the page.

1. Demonstrate
Demonstrate **p** on the Blackboard with Double Lines, whiteboard, or flip chart.
Use "Diver Letters' School," track 18, *Rock, Rap, Tap & Learn* CD.
Children finger trace the large lowercase **p** model in their workbooks.

2. Copy
Prepare for writing with good posture, pencil grip, and use of the helper hand.
Demonstrate **p** again, saying the step-by-step directions together.
Children watch, then copy **p**'s.

3. Check & Evaluate
Help children ☑ their letter for correct Start, Steps, and Bump.
Evaluate the correct formation for lowercase **p**.

Read, Color & Draw
Read the sentence together. Point out the beginning of capital **P** and the lowercase **p**'s in puppies.
Encourage free coloring and drawing. Add grass, a ball, etc.

More to Learn
Use "Descending Letters," track 19, *Rock, Rap, Tap & Learn* CD for **g**, **j**, **y**, **p**, and **q**.

Support/ELL
Help children retrace neatly by highlighting the line down of each **p**. Children stay on your highlighted line as they trace down and up to begin **p**.

CONNECTIONS

Language Arts Link: Listen to different animal sounds.
What sounds do puppies make? Have children tell
different animals apart by the noises animals make.

Words & Sentence for Me

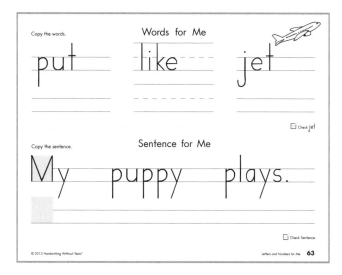

OBJECTIVE: To practice writing words and a sentence correctly.

Lesson Plan

Help children turn to p. 63. Read the words and sentence together.

1. **Demonstrate the words for children to copy.**
   Prepare double lines for **put**, triple lines for **like**, and double lines for **jet**.
   Demonstrate **put**, **like**, and **jet**. Children copy all words.

2. **Demonstrate the sentence for children to copy.**
   Prepare double lines.
   Use "Sentence Song," track 7, *Rock, Rap, Tap & Learn* CD.
   Demonstrate **My puppy plays.** for children to copy.

3. **Check & Evaluate**
   Help children ✓ their word for correct Size, Placement, and Closeness.
   Help children ✓ their sentence for correct Capitalization, Word Spacing, and Ending Punctuation.
   Evaluate children as they copy the words and sentence, and help them as needed.

Read, Color & Draw

Read the words and sentence together.
Encourage free coloring and drawing. You may show, step by step, how to draw a puppy face.

More to Learn

Use The Hand Activity (p. 104) to develop awareness of tall, small, and descending letters.

Support/ELL

Support good sentence spacing by showing children how to use two fingers to add spaces between words.

CONNECTIONS

Language Arts Link: Play with beginning sounds using **p** while writing sentences. Example, "Pam's pet parrot is playful." Practice writing with previously learned letters.

r

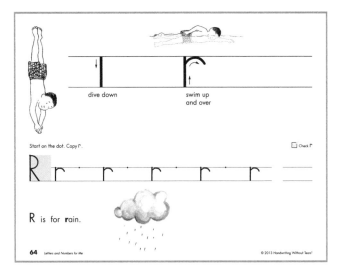

OBJECTIVE: To write lowercase **r** with correct formation.

Lesson Plan
Let's find the lowercase r page. Help children turn to p. 64. Discuss what's on the page.

1. Demonstrate
Demonstrate **r** on the Blackboard with Double Lines, whiteboard, or flip chart.
Use "Diver Letters' School," track 18, *Rock, Rap, Tap & Learn* CD.
Children finger trace the large lowercase **r** model in their workbooks.

2. Copy
Prepare for writing with good posture, pencil grip, and use of the helper hand.
Demonstrate **r** again, saying the step-by-step directions together.
Children watch, then copy **r**'s.

3. Check & Evaluate
Help children ☑ their letter for correct Start, Steps, and Bump.
Evaluate the correct formation for lowercase **r**.

Read, Color & Draw
Read the sentence together. Point out the beginning of capital **R** and the lowercase **r** in rain.
Encourage free coloring and drawing. Add a rainbow, rain drops, etc.

More to Learn
The Diver Letters **p**, **r**, **n**, **m**, **h**, and **b** begin with a "dive down, swim up" stroke. Show underwater films that show how Olympic divers "swim up" in their bubbles.

Support/ELL
Highlighting the "dive down" stroke for Diver Letters helps children retrace. They stay on the highlighted line. Acting out the Diver Letters (p. 109) makes for inclusive learning.

CONNECTIONS

Language Arts Link: Read non-fiction books about rain and discuss why it's important. What else do children know about rain? Write a class story about rain.

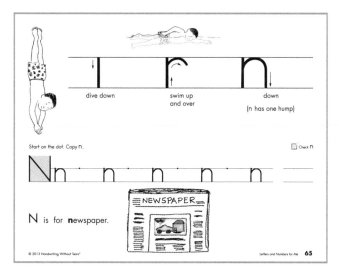

dive down   + swim up and over   + down

n

Start on the dot. Copy n.

Check n

N n   n   n   n   n

N is for **n**ewspaper.

NEWSPAPER

© 2013 Handwriting Without Tears®

Letters and Numbers for Me **65**

OBJECTIVE: To write lowercase **n** with correct formation.

Lesson Plan
Let's find the lowercase n page. Help children turn to p. 65. Discuss what's on the page.

1. Demonstrate
Demonstrate **n** on the Blackboard with Double Lines, whiteboard, or flip chart.
Use Air Writing for **n** (multisensory activity p. 61).
Children finger trace the large lowercase **n** model in their workbooks.

2. Copy
Prepare for writing with good posture, pencil grip, and use of the helper hand.
Demonstrate **n** again, saying the step-by-step directions together.
Children watch, then copy **n**'s.

3. Check & Evaluate
Help children ☑ their letter for correct Start, Steps, and Bump.
Evaluate the correct formation for lowercase **n**.

Read, Color & Draw
Read the sentence together. Point out the beginning of capital **N** and the lowercase **n** in newspaper.
Encourage free coloring and drawing. Add a picture you might see in the newspaper.

More to Learn
For the top of **n**, show children how to travel on the mid line before turning down (this also works for **m**, **h**, and **b**). This produces neat letters and it's fun to do.

Support/ELL
Reread the lowercase letter pages together starting with p. 40 in the workbook. Do not read past lowercase **n**.

CONNECTIONS

🏠 **Home Link:** Have children read a newspaper at home with their families. To download this activity, visit **hwtears.com/click**

m

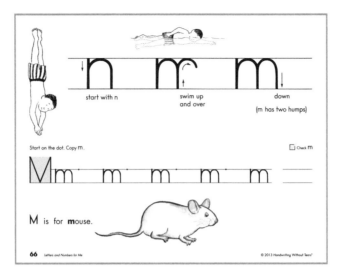

OBJECTIVE: To write lowercase **m** with correct formation.

Lesson Plan
Let's find the lowercase m page. Help children turn to p. 66. Discuss what's on the page.

1. Demonstrate
Demonstrate **m** on the Blackboard with Double Lines, whiteboard, or flip chart.
Use Letter Story for **m** (multisensory activity p. 107).
Children finger trace the large lowercase **m** model in their workbooks.

2. Copy
Prepare for writing with good posture, pencil grip, and use of the helper hand.
Demonstrate **m** again, saying the step-by-step directions together.
Children watch, then copy **m**'s.

3. Check & Evaluate
Help children ☑ their letter for correct Start, Steps, and Bump.
Evaluate the correct formation for lowercase **m**.

Read, Color & Draw
Read the sentence together. Point out the beginning of capital **M** and the lowercase **m** in mouse.
Encourage free coloring and drawing. Add cheese, grass, etc.

More to Learn
Use Air Writing for **m** (p. 61). When facing children, make the letter backwards for you (start on your right), so it will be correct for them.

Support/ELL
Use Wet-Dry-Try for **m** on the Blackboard with Double Lines (p. 105).

CONNECTIONS

Math Link: Read "Hickory Dickory Dock."
Where does the mouse run? Discuss clocks and the concept of time.

Words & Sentence for Me

OBJECTIVE: To practice writing words and a sentence correctly.

Lesson Plan

Help children turn to p. 67. Read the words and sentence together.

1. **Demonstrate the words for children to copy.**
   Prepare double lines for **run**, triple lines for **and**, and double lines for **net**.
   Demonstrate **run**, **and**, and **net**. Children copy all the words.

2. **Demonstrate the sentence for children to copy.**
   Prepare double lines.
   Demonstrate **Pam saw a mouse.** for children to copy.

3. **Check & Evaluate**
   Help children ☑ their word for correct Size, Placement, and Closeness.
   Help children ☑ their sentence for correct Capitalization, Word Spacing, and Ending Punctuation.
   Evaluate children as they copy the words and sentence, and help them as needed.

Read, Color & Draw

Read the words and sentence together.
Encourage free coloring and drawing.

More to Learn

Give a "bump the lines" challenge. Every lowercase letter in "Pam saw a mouse." is small and should bump the mid line and base line.

Support/ELL

Slowly read and spell the words together to promote left-to-right tracking and letter naming. Many letters (**a**, **d**, **e**, **m**, **n**, **r**) are not similar to their capital partners.

CONNECTIONS

Language Arts Link: As a story starter, use the sentence, "Pam saw a mouse." Have children write or draw a picture about what happens next.

dive down   + swim up and over   + down

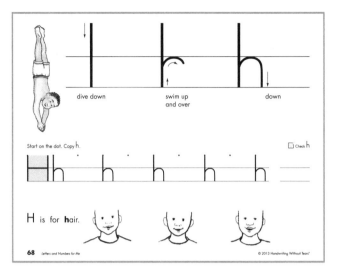

OBJECTIVE: To write lowercase **h** with correct formation.

Lesson Plan
Let's find the lowercase h page. Help children turn to p. 68. Discuss what's on the page.

1. **Demonstrate**
   Demonstrate **h** on the Blackboard with Double Lines, whiteboard, or flip chart.
   Use "Diver Letters' School," track 18, *Rock, Rap, Tap & Learn* CD.
   Children finger trace the large lowercase **h** model in their workbooks.

2. **Copy**
   Prepare for writing with good posture, pencil grip, and use of the helper hand.
   Demonstrate **h** again, saying the step-by-step directions together.
   Children watch, then copy **h**'s.

3. **Check & Evaluate**
   Help children ☑ their letter for correct Start, Steps, and Bump.
   Evaluate the correct formation for lowercase **h**.

Read, Color & Draw
Read the sentence together. Point out the beginning of capital **H** and the lowercase **h** in hair.
Encourage free coloring and drawing. Add different types of hair, different hair colors, etc.

More to Learn
Make a class list of things that rhyme with hair. Provide a few examples and then see if children can come up with their own.

Support/ELL
For the top of **h**, show children how to travel on the mid line before turning down. This produces neat letters and it's fun to do.

CONNECTIONS

Math Link: Make a pictograph of the different hair lengths in your classroom. Children can count and compare the results.

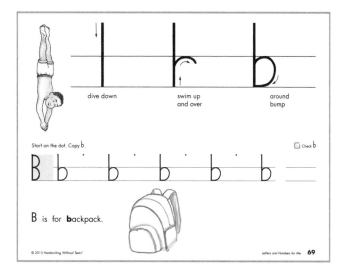

OBJECTIVE: To write lowercase **b** with correct formation.

Lesson Plan
Let's find the lowercase b page. Help children turn to p. 69. Discuss what's on the page.

1. Demonstrate
Demonstrate **b** on the Blackboard with Double Lines, whiteboard, or flip chart.
Use Letter Story for **b** (multisensory activity p. 106).
Children finger trace the large lowercase **b** model in their workbooks.

2. Copy
Prepare for writing with good posture, pencil grip, and use of the helper hand.
Demonstrate **b** again, saying the step-by-step directions together.
Children watch, then copy **b**'s.

3. Check & Evaluate
Help children ☑ their letter for correct Start, Steps, and Bump.
Evaluate the correct formation for lowercase **b**.

Read, Color & Draw
Read the sentence together. Point out the beginning of capital **B** and the lowercase **b** in backpack.
Encourage free coloring and drawing. Add items for the backpack.

More to Learn
Bring in a backpack full of items (some that start with **b** and some that don't). Place items on the floor. Allow children to place items starting with **b** in the backpack.

Support/ELL
Letter **b** uses the same beginning strokes as **h**. Letter **h** is very seldom reversed. Teaching children to write **h** and turn **h** into **b** avoids confusion.

CONNECTIONS

Language Arts Link: Backpack is a compound word. Explain compound words and discuss other compound words (cupcake, fishbowl, football, etc).

🏠 **Home Link:** This is the end of the Diver Letters Group **p**, **r**, **n**, **m**, **h**, and **b**. A description of these letters and home practice is available at **hwtears.com/click**

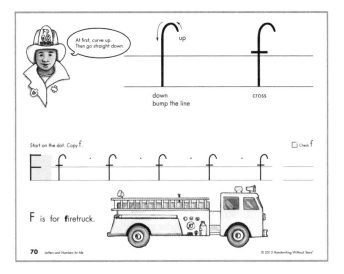

At first, curve up. Then go straight down.

up

down
bump the line

cross

Start on the dot. Copy f.

☐ Check f

F f   f   f   f   f

F is for firetruck.

70 *Letters and Numbers for Me*

© 2013 Handwriting Without Tears®

OBJECTIVE: To write lowercase **f** with correct formation.

Lesson Plan
Let's find the lowercase f page. Help children turn to p. 70. Discuss what's on the page.

1. Demonstrate
Demonstrate **f** on the Blackboard with Double Lines, whiteboard, or flip chart.
Use Letter Story for **f** (multisensory activity p. 106).
Children finger trace the large lowercase **f** model in their workbooks.

2. Copy
Prepare for writing with good posture, pencil grip, and use of the helper hand.
Demonstrate **f** again, saying the step-by-step directions together.
Children watch, then copy **f**'s.

3. Check & Evaluate
Help children ☑ their letter for correct Start, Steps, and Bump.
Evaluate the correct formation for lowercase **f**.

Read, Color & Draw
Read the sentence together. Point out the beginning of capital **F** and the lowercase **f** in firetruck.
Encourage free coloring and drawing. Add a road, a tree, water hose, etc.

More to Learn
Review the starting positions of lowercase **f** and **e**.
They are the only exceptions to the rule to start
your letters at the top.

Support/ELL
Help left-handed children with crossing **f**. It is natural and
easier for lefties to pull from right to left. Draw an arrow
on the model as a reminder.

CONNECTIONS

Social Studies Link: Discuss the fire station,
public library, police station, hospital, and post office.
Identify how these services help the community.

Words & Sentence for Me

OBJECTIVE: To practice writing words and a sentence correctly.

Lesson Plan
Help children turn to p. 71. Read the words and sentence together.

1. **Demonstrate the words for children to copy.**
   Prepare double lines for **beef**, triple lines for **bath**, and double lines for **fish**.
   Demonstrate **beef**, **bath**, and **fish**. Children copy all words.

2. **Demonstrate the sentence for children to copy.**
   Prepare double lines.
   Demonstrate **Jeff is very brave.** for children to copy.

3. **Check & Evaluate**
   Help children ☑ their word for correct Size, Placement, and Closeness.
   Help children ☑ their sentence for correct Capitalization, Word Spacing, and Ending Punctuation.
   Evaluate children as they copy the words and sentence, and help them as needed.

Read, Color & Draw
Read the words and sentence together.
Encourage free coloring and drawing. Children may like to draw Jeff.

More to Learn
Double lines are easier for children to follow, because two lines are easier to follow than three or four. Use Wide Double Line Notebook Paper to write sentences.

Support/ELL
Review letter **e** separately before the lesson. Letter **e** is challenging and there are five **e**'s to copy on the workbook page.

CONNECTIONS

Language Arts Link: Discuss what it means to be brave. Read books about a character who is brave and have children make connections to bravery.

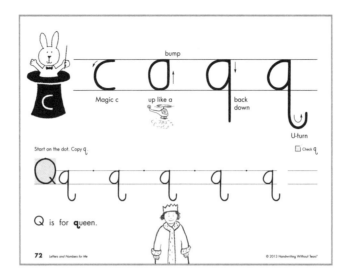

Start on the dot. Copy q   ☐ Check q

Q is for **q**ueen.

72   *Letters and Numbers for Me*   © 2013 Handwriting Without Tears®

OBJECTIVE: To write lowercase **q** with correct formation.

Lesson Plan
Let's find the lowercase q page. Help children turn to p. 72. Discuss what's on the page.

1. Demonstrate
Demonstrate **q** on the Blackboard with Double Lines, whiteboard, or flip chart.
Use Letter Story for **q** (multisensory activity p. 107).
Children finger trace the large lowercase **q** model in their workbooks.

2. Copy
Prepare for writing with good posture, pencil grip, and use of the helper hand.
Demonstrate **q** again, saying the step-by-step directions together.
Children watch, then copy **q**'s.

3. Check & Evaluate
Help children ☑ their letter for correct Start, Steps, and Bump.
Evaluate the correct formation for lowercase **q**.

Read, Color & Draw
Read the sentence together. Point out the beginning of capital **Q** and the lowercase **q** in queen.
Encourage free coloring and drawing. Add a king, a castle, etc.

More to Learn
Use "Descending Letters," track 19, *Rock, Rap, Tap & Learn* CD for **g, j, y, p,** and **q**.

Support/ELL
The letter **q** is always followed by **u**. Teach children to finish **q** with a U-turn so they can practice writing the next letter in the word.

CONNECTIONS

Social Studies Link: Talk about queens around the world. What do queens do? Where do queens live?

X

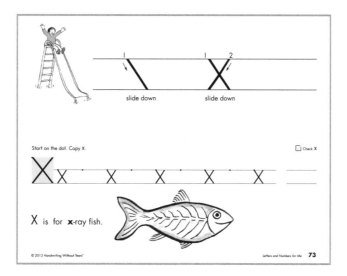

OBJECTIVE: To write lowercase **x** with correct formation.

Lesson Plan
Let's find the lowercase x page. Help children turn to p. 73. Discuss what's on the page.

1. Demonstrate
Demonstrate **x** on the Blackboard with Double Lines, whiteboard, or flip chart.
Use "Sliding Down to the End of the Alphabet," track 15, *Rock, Rap, Tap & Learn* CD.
Children finger trace the large lowercase **x** model in their workbooks.

2. Copy
Prepare for writing with good posture, pencil grip, and use of the helper hand.
Demonstrate **x** again, saying the step-by-step directions together.
Children watch, then copy **x**'s.

3. Check & Evaluate
Help children ☑ their letter for correct Start, Steps, and Bump.
Evaluate the correct formation for lowercase **x**.

Read, Color & Draw
Read the sentence together. Point out the beginning of capital **X** and the lowercase **x** in x-ray fish.
Encourage free coloring and drawing. Help children draw water and other fish.

More to Learn
Another song children enjoy for learning **x** is "Diagonals,"
track 5, *Rock, Rap, Tap & Learn* CD.

Support/ELL
Left-handed children often need support to begin **x** at the
top left. Others may, too. Highlight the first slide down
stroke to trace.

CONNECTIONS

Science Link: Read informational books about fish.
Discuss and identify the parts of a fish. Label the parts
of a fish on an easel or whiteboard as a class

go across   + slide down   + go across

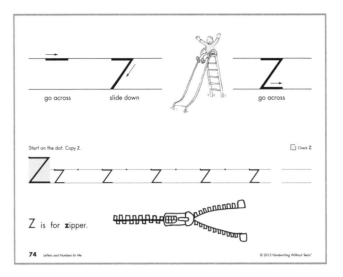

OBJECTIVE: To write lowercase **z** with correct formation.

Lesson Plan
Let's find the lowercase z page. Help children turn to p. 74. Discuss what's on the page.

1. Demonstrate
Demonstrate **z** on the Blackboard with Double Lines, whiteboard, or flip chart.
Use Letter Story for **z** (multisensory activity p. 107).
Children finger trace the large lowercase **z** model in their workbooks.

2. Copy
Prepare for writing with good posture, pencil grip, and use of the helper hand.
Demonstrate **z** again, saying the step-by-step directions together.
Children watch, then copy **z**'s.

3. Check & Evaluate
Help children ☑ their letter for correct Start, Steps, and Bump.
Evaluate the correct formation for lowercase **z**.

Read, Color & Draw
Read the sentence together. Point out the beginning of capital **Z** and the lowercase **z** in zipper.
Encourage free coloring and drawing. Add a zipper tag, clothes, etc.

More to Learn
Use Air Writing for **z** (p. 61). When facing children, make **z** backwards for you (start on your right), so **z** will be correct for them.

Support/ELL
Whenever a child has difficulty with a lowercase letter that has a similar capital partner: **c**, **o**, **s**, **v**, **w**, **x**, and **z** use Wet-Dry-Try on the Slate Chalkboard (p. 59).

CONNECTIONS

Math Link: Count or graph how many children in the room have zippers on their coats? How many have buttons? How many have both?

Copy the words. Words for Me

quiz   fuzz   fox

☐ Check fox

Copy the sentence. Sentence for Me

Zebras   run   fast.

☐ Check Sentence

© 2013 Handwriting Without Tears® *Letters and Numbers for Me* **75**

OBJECTIVE: To practice writing words and a sentence correctly.

Lesson Plan
Help children turn to p. 75. Read the words and sentence together.

1. Demonstrate the words for children to copy.
Prepare double lines for **quiz**, triple lines for **fuzz**, and double lines for **fox**.
Demonstrate **quiz**, **fuzz**, and **fox**. Children copy all words.

2. Demonstrate the sentence for children to copy.
Prepare double lines.
Use "Sentence Song," track 7, *Rock, Rap, Tap & Learn* CD.
Demonstrate **Zebras   run   fast.** for children to copy.

3. Check & Evaluate
Help children ☑ their word for correct Size, Placement, and Closeness.
Help children ☑ their sentence for correct Capitalization, Word Spacing, and Ending Punctuation.
Evaluate children as they copy the words and sentence, and help them as needed.

Read, Color & Draw
Read the words and sentence together.
Encourage free coloring and drawing.

More to Learn
Discuss other animals that run fast. Write sentences using the animals in place of "zebra." For example, discuss tigers and then write the sentence, "Tigers run fast."

Support/ELL
Slowly read and spell the words together to promote left-to-right tracking and letter naming. Many letters (**a, b, e, f, i, n, q**) are not familiar from capitals.

CONNECTIONS

Science Link: Besides zebras, what other animals can run fast? What animals are slow? Have children create a list of animals in each category and write sentences.

🏠 Home Link: This is the end of the Final Group **f, q, x**, and **z**. A description of these letters and home practice is available at **hwtears.com/click**

Magic c Mystery Letters

MAGIC c MYSTERY LETTERS

Change c into a, d, g, o, or q.

Start on the dot.
Trace c.
Don't lift your pencil.
Wait for the mystery letter.

OBJECTIVE: To solidify good habits and change poor ones (wrong formation, reversals, floating letters).

Lesson Plan
Help children turn to p. 76. Read the title. Explain that a mystery is like a secret. **We will start letters, before we know what letter we're writing. Each letter will be a mystery.**

1. **Preview the activity on the board, letting children play "teacher."**
   Prepare the board like the first line.
   Play the child's part, following the directions on p. 76.
   Say to first child, **Tell me a Mystery Letter. Choose a, d, g, o, or q.**
   Turn Magic c into the child's Mystery Letter. Repeat, letting more children be the teacher.

2. **Do one line of the Magic c Mystery Letters game.**
   Children follow the teacher's directions:
   > **Start on the dot. Trace c.**
   > **Don't lift your pencil. Wait for the Mystery Letter.**
   > **Turn Magic c into the Mystery Letter.** (Name any Magic c Letter.)
   Repeat until the line is finished.

3. **Monitor as children write Magic c Mystery Letters.**
   Make sure children wait at the bottom of each **c** for the Mystery Letter to be named.

More to Learn
Try this activity on the Blackboard with Double Lines (p. 105). The larger scale and tactile component add variety to this important activity.

Support/ELL
You can change habits if you change the stimulus. Not knowing the letter name (old stimulus) prevents using old letter habits. New stimulus = new response and new habits.

CONNECTIONS

▶ **Video Lesson:** View "Magic c Mystery Letters" at hwtears.com/videos

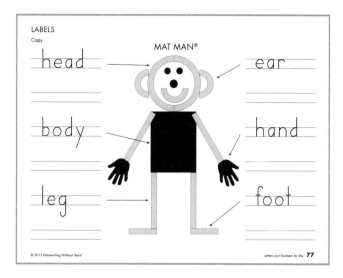

OBJECTIVE: To learn about labels, while reviewing body parts with a favorite activity.

Lesson Plan

Help children turn to p. 77. Read the title. Read the words together.

1. **Demonstrate how words work as labels.**
   Draw Mat Man® on the board. **This is a picture of Mat Man.**
   Prepare double lines near the head.
   Write the word **head**. Explain that **head** is a label for that body part in the picture.
   Children copy the word **head** in their workbooks.

2. **Demonstrate more labels for children to copy.**
   Prepare two sets of double lines on the board.
   Demonstrate **ear** and **body**.
   Children copy all labels for body parts.

3. **Monitor as children copy the labels.**
   Walk around the room as children copy. Help or teach again as needed.

More to Learn
Review body parts with "Mat Man Rock," track 23, *Rock, Rap, Tap & Learn* CD.

Support/ELL
Build Mat Man (pp. 28–29) again. Encourage students to use vocabulary and make connections between Mat Man's body parts and their own.

CONNECTIONS

Math Link: Count Mat Man's body parts. Count his head, eyes, ears, nose, hands, mouth, legs, and feet. How many body parts does he have?

Punctuation

PUNCTUATION
Copy the punctuation marks.

Periods   Question marks   Exclamation points

Copy the sentences on the triple lines.

Is this a question?

It is. I knew it!

78 *Letters and Numbers for Me*   © 2013 Handwriting Without Tears®

OBJECTIVE: To write and use periods, question marks, and exclamation points correctly.

Lesson Plan
Help children turn to p. 78. Read the names of the punctuation marks. Read sentences together.

1. **Demonstrate punctuation marks for children to copy.**
   Use "Sentence Song," track 7, *Rock, Rap, Tap & Learn* CD to review ending punctuation.
   Prepare single lines on blackboard, whiteboard, or flip chart.
   Demonstrate periods, question marks, and exclamation points.
   Children copy.

2. **Demonstrate the first sentence for children to copy.**
   Prepare triple lines on the board.
   Demonstrate **Is this a question?**
   Children copy the sentences.

3. **Monitor as children copy the sentences.**
   Watch and help as needed with sentence skills, especially ending punctuation.

More to Learn
Discuss how our voices and faces change if sentences are statements, questions, or have strong emotion. When we write, punctuation shows what kind of sentence it is.

Support/ELL
Model each sentence, word by word if needed. Use facial expressions with the words, statements, questions, and exclamations. It's fun to make faces together and say words.

CONNECTIONS

Language Arts Link: Consider using *Mrs. Wishy Washy* by Joy Cowley and take children on a punctuation trip through the book.

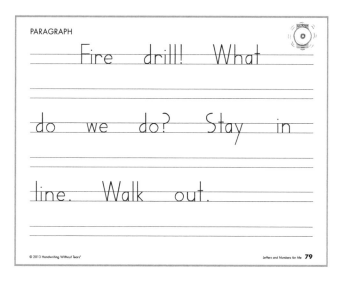

OBJECTIVES: To learn about paragraphs; to practice punctuation.

Lesson Plan

Help children turn to p. 79. Read the paragraph. Discuss the topic. Fire Drill! is not a sentence. It's an exclamation. The sentences are about a fire drill. That's the topic of the paragraph.

1. **Demonstrate "Fire Drill!" for children to copy.**
   Prepare double lines on the board.
   Introduce the word "indent." **We indent (start with a space) to begin a paragraph.**
   Demonstrate how to indent **Fire Drill!**
   Children copy.

2. **Demonstrate "What" for children to copy.**
   Leave a space after "Fire Drill!"
   Demonstrate "**What**" for children to copy.
   Explain that the question, "What do we do?" continues on the next line.
   Children copy the rest of the paragraph.

3. **Monitor as children copy the paragraph.**
   Watch and help as needed.
   Demonstrate line by line if that makes the lesson more effective.

More to Learn

Show books with indented paragraphs to children. Find the indents and paragraphs. Just like sentences, paragraphs can go from page to page!

Support/ELL

Take three days to do this page. Read the paragraph from the beginning each day. Explain each part. Review indentation and punctuation.

CONNECTIONS

Social Studies Link: Talk about following rules. It's important to follow rules in order to keep our community safe. Can children identify other safety rules?

Rhymes

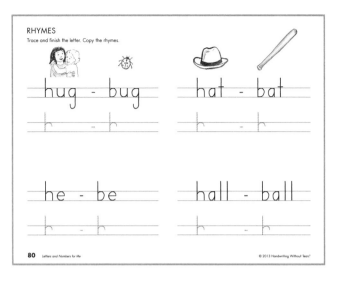

OBJECTIVES: To develop word fluency with rhyming words; to practice letter formation for **h** and **b**.

Lesson Plan
Help children turn to p. 80. Read the words together. Ask children about the first letters of each word pair. Listen for the rhymes.

1. **Demonstrate how to change letter h into b.**
   Use Air Writing for **h** and **b** (multisensory activity p. 61).
   Make **h** in the air for children to follow.
   Repeat, saying, **"This is an h, for a honeybee. I turn h into b."**
   Teacher demonstrates.

2. **Demonstrate "hug-bug" for children to copy.**
   Preview placement with The Hand Activity (multisensory activity p. 104).
   Demonstrate "**hug - bug**," pointing out that **h** and **b** begin the same way.
   Explain that rhymes have the same ending sound.
   Children copy the rest of the rhymes.

3. **Monitor as children copy the rhyming words.**
   Watch and help children as needed with word skills: Size, Placement, Closeness.

More to Learn
Use Wide Double Line Paper for extra **h** and **b** rhyming practice. You write the h word on the board and they write the **b** words (examples: hut, hit, hill, had, hand).

Support/ELL
Practice pointing to and reading the words together from top to bottom and left to right. The rhyming makes it easier for children to join.

CONNECTIONS

Language Arts Link: Say or read familiar nursery rhymes. See if children can add their own rhyming word.

OBJECTIVE: To write a short simple poem, beginning each new line with a capital.

Lesson Plan

Help children turn to p. 81. Teach poem basics: title, rhyme, and lines. Find the title at the top: "A Spider." Read the poem and listen for rhymes. Look at the poem and find the lines.

1. **Demonstrate the first line for children to copy.**
   Prepare double lines on the board.
   Demonstrate **Oh dear** for children to copy.
   Demonstrate the **!** exclamation point. Children copy.

2. **Demonstrate the next line for children to copy.**
   Explain that poems use lines not sentences. Each new thought has its own line.
   Demonstrate **Spider near** for children to copy.
   Demonstrate the comma (**,**). Children copy the rest of the poem.

3. **Monitor as children copy the poem.**
   Watch and help as needed, especially with the punctuation.

More to Learn

Look at poetry books. Look at the lines. How do they start (capital)? Where do they start (own line)? How do they end (commas, questions, exclamations, and periods)?

Support/ELL

Simple poems are excellent for teaching top-to-bottom, left-to-right tracking. Copying very short poems boosts fluency because rhymes often repeat the same ending letters.

CONNECTIONS

Language Arts Link: Discuss the different elements of a poem. This poem is inspired by "Little Miss Muffet." Write a class poem.

Greetings

82 Letters and Numbers for Me © 2013 Handwriting Without Tears®

OBJECTIVES: To practice copying on single lines; to introduce quotes as spoken words.

Lesson Plan
Help children turn to p. 82. Introduce these children to your students. Have your students return the greetings. **Tanya says, "Hello." Ming says, "Ni hao." Ramona says, "Hola." Pierre says, "Bonjour."**

1. **Introduce quotes as spoken words.**
   Have children point to Tanya and the word "Hello."
   Explain that quote bubbles hold the words people say.
   Explain that quotation marks also hold the words people say.

2. **Demonstrate "Hello" on a single line.**
   Preview placement with The Hand Activity (multisensory activity p. 104).
   Demonstrate **"Hello."** on the board for children to copy.
   Children copy the rest of the words from the quote bubbles.

3. **Monitor as children finish the sentences.**
   Watch and help children copy words as needed from the quote bubbles.

More to Learn
Check and teach pronunciation of the Chinese, Spanish, and French greetings. Show quote bubbles in comic books or comic pages. Look for quotation marks in children's books.

Support/ELL
Writing on a single line is tricky. If needed, add a mid line.

CONNECTIONS

Social Studies Link: Use a map to identify where children are from. Explain there are many ways to say hello. Ask if the children know another way.

More Sentences

Copying modeled sentences regularly helps children carry skills into their independent sentence writing. Use the Sentence School® product (p. 189) or follow these suggestions to bring your own sentences to life.

Materials
- Random objects
- Double Line Notebook Paper
- *Rock, Rap, Tap & Learn* CD, "Sentence Song," track 7

Grouping
Whole class

Support/ELL
Adjust seating for children who need help, by placing them close to you and with a direct view of the board. Review sentence basics with "Sentence Song."

Activity

1. Engage students with a physical action or a real object.
   Action: line up, pass, wash, stretch, sing, move, reach, jump, etc.
   Object: something big/little, rough/smooth, heavy/light, shiny/dull, etc.

2. Make up a sentence together about their experience. For example:
   Talk about the action: **I wash my hands.**
   Talk about the object: **Soap is slippery.**
   Ask about the experience: **What else do we wash?**

3. Demonstrate the sentence for children to copy.

✓ Check
Observe children as they copy the sentences. Are children applying their sentence writing skills both when they copy and in independent writing?

More to Learn
Sentences with strong emotions end with exclamation points. Explain that exclamations are not always sentences (e.g., Wow!).

CONNECTIONS

Language Arts Link: Write sentences on the board as a class. Write an action sentence, a describing sentence, and a question. Discuss how they are different.

NUMBERS

Let's talk about numbers. If you're new to Handwriting Without Tears®, you are in for a surprise. You can joyfully and efficiently teach your students to write numbers correctly! That means numbers that start at the top, use the right strokes, and face correctly.

What about reversals? Not a problem! Our materials and strategies work to prevent letter and number reversal problems. When we use these strategies for kindergartners, reversals are never a problem.

Why do children make reversals? It's simply because they're making a transition from learning in the real world to the world of symbols. In the real world, they learned that position doesn't affect identity. A person is still the same person if they turn to face a different way. An upside down chair is still a chair. That's the real world.

But letters and numbers are symbols and the real world rules don't apply. In the symbol world of letters and numbers, position matters. A change in position changes meaning and identity. Letter **M** isn't **W**. Letter **b** isn't **d**. Number **6** isn't **9**. Welcome children to the world of symbols! Typically, it's confusing. But with our materials and strategies, you can help children transition smoothly into the world of symbols for school success.

You can easily teach your kindergartners to write numbers correctly. That's something to smile about! And guess what? A smiley face in the top left corner of the Slate Chalkboard or Gray Block does the trick. The smiley face orients children. When the face is right side up, the number is right side up. When numbers **1**, **2**, **3**, **4**, **5**, **6**, and **7** start by the smiley face (top left corner) they face correctly. Numbers **8** and **9** are exceptions. They have their own starting places, and they're easy to learn, too. Number **10** is taught as numbers **1** and **0**.

Teaching Numbers

Teaching numbers is satisfying. Lessons are visual, auditory, tactile, kinesthetic, and never boring. The Slate Chalkboard, Gray Blocks, stories, and songs make learning appealing and effective. Expect excellence!

 The smiley face shows the top left corner. The smiley face helps children orient numbers. The frame gives children a practical frame of reference.

Numbers on the Slate Chalkboard

1, 2, 3, 4, 5, 6, and **7** start at the ☺ in the Starting Corner. When they start there, they are never reversed. Number **8** is a Center Starter and begins like capital **S**. Number **9** is so special—it has its own corner.

Numbers on the Gray Blocks

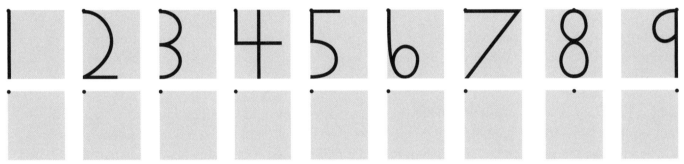

The Gray Blocks represent the inside of the Slate Chalkboard. With Gray Blocks, we transition to pencil and paper.

Number Stories & More

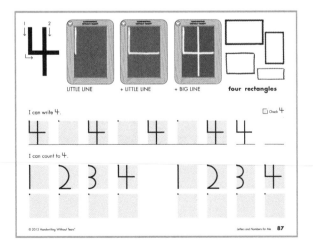

After children have previewed new numbers on the Slate Chalkboard, they're ready for workbook lessons. Here's how the workbook pages help you teach:

- Numbers large enough for finger tracing
- Numbers on the Slate Chalkboard
- Things to count and color
- Number words to read
- Numbers to copy on Gray Blocks

Wet-Dry-Try for Numbers

This activity appeals to the senses! Children eagerly watch you write the number, waiting for their part. They get to wet the number with a Little Sponge Cube, and trace the number with a wet finger. Then, they trace it dry with a towel. Finally, they try it with a Little Chalk Bit. The wetting and drying make practicing correct formation a pure delight.

Materials
- Slate Chalkboard (1 per child)
- Little Chalk Bits (1")
- Little Sponge Cubes (1/2")
- Little cups of water
- Paper towel pieces

Grouping
Small group

Support/ELL
Say the words for each step slowly. Children join when they can. Encourage children to repeat after you.

Activity

1. **Teacher's Part – Write 4 with Chalk**
   Use chalk to write a letter on the Slate Chalkboard.
   Say the step-by-step directions.

2. **Child's Part – Wet-Dry-Try**
   As the child does each part, say the step-by-step directions to guide the child. The child is encouraged to join in, saying the words.
   Wet: The child uses a Little Sponge Cube to trace the letter.
   Dry: The child uses a little piece of paper towel to trace the letter.
   Try: The child uses a Little Chalk Bit to write the number.

✔ Check
Observe how children place their Slate Chalkboards. Do all children have their Slate Chalkboards placed vertically with the ☺ at the top?

More to Learn
Review previously learned numbers 1, 2, and 3 with chalk. Demonstrate on the Slate Chalkboard. Children imitate on their Slate Chalkboards. Erase with a crumbled paper towel.

Teacher's Part

Start in the Starting Corner,
Little Line down,
Little Line across, jump to top,
Big Line down

Child's Part

WET:
Wet 4 with sponge,
Wet 4 with wet finger,
Say the words

DRY:
Dry 4 with towel,
Dry 4 with gentle blow,
Say the words

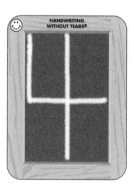

TRY:
Try 4 with chalk,
Say the words

CONNECTIONS

⏻ **Technology Link:** To teach numbers with large movements, visit our Digital Teaching Tools at **hwtears.com/dtt**

Number Stories

Fun stories help children remember numbers. Beyond our simple verbal cues, we made up stories that are fun to share and help make these numbers memorable.

1 starts in the Starting Corner.

1 makes a Big Line down.

1 stops in the corner.

6 starts in the Starting Corner.

6 is a baby bear.

6 goes down to curl up in the corner.

6 is hibernating.

2 starts in the Starting Corner.

2 makes a Big Curve.

2 stops in the corner.

2 walks away on the bottom.

7 starts in the Starting Corner.

7 makes a Little Line across the top.

7 says, "I better slide down."

3 starts in the Starting Corner.

3 makes a Little Curve to the middle.

3 makes another Little Curve to the bottom corner.

8 is different.

8 doesn't like corners.

8 starts at the top center.

8 begins with **S** and then goes home.

4 starts in the Starting Corner.

4 makes a Little Line down to the middle.

4 walks across the dark night.

4 jumps to the top and says, "I did it." (Big Line down)

9 is so special.

9 has its own corner.

9 makes a Little Curve and goes up to the corner.

9 makes a Big Line down.

5 starts in the Starting Corner.

5 makes a Little Line down to the middle. It starts to rain.

5 makes a Little Curve around.

5 puts a Little Line on top to stop the rain.

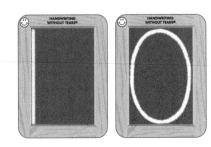

10 uses two places.

1 comes first.

0 is next.

0 starts at the top center.

10 is finished.

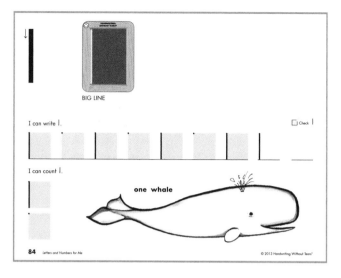

OBJECTIVE: To write number **I** with correct formation.

Lesson Plan
Let's find the number I page. Help children turn to p. 84. Discuss what's on the page.
One starts at the top in the Starting Corner ☺. Have children point to the Starting Corner.

1. Demonstrate
Demonstrate **I** on the Slate Chalkboard, whiteboard, or flip chart.
Use Wet-Dry-Try on the Slate Chalkboard for **I** (multisensory activity p. 159).
Children finger trace the large number **I** in their workbooks.

2. Copy
Prepare for writing with good posture, pencil grip, and use of the helper hand.
Demonstrate **I** again on the Slate Chalkboard, saying the step-by-step directions together.
Children watch, then copy **I**'s.

3. Check & Evaluate
Help children ☑ their number for correct Start, Steps, and Bump.
Evaluate the correct formation for number **I**.

Read, Color & Draw
Read the label: **one whale**. Read the sentences: **I can write I. I can count I.**
Encourage free coloring and drawing. Add water, small fish, etc.

More to Learn
Some children come to kindergarten making **1** with a top and bottom. Gently discourage that formation. Keep **I** simple.

Support/ELL
Some children come to kindergarten starting numbers from the base line. Encourage them to start at the top. Remind them that numbers, like letters, start at the top.

CONNECTIONS

Math Link: Teach children about one-to-one correspondence. Have children pass out objects to each student and use phrases like, "One crayon for you."

BIG CURVE + LITTLE LINE

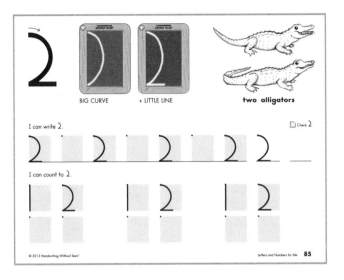

OBJECTIVE: To write number 2 with correct formation.

Lesson Plan
Let's find the number 2 page. Help children turn to p. 85. Discuss what's on the page.
Two starts at the top in the Starting Corner ☺. Have children point to the Starting Corner.

1. Demonstrate
Demonstrate 2 on the Slate Chalkboard, whiteboard, or flip chart.
Use Wet-Dry-Try on the Slate Chalkboard for 2 (multisensory activity p. 159).
Children finger trace the large number 2 in their workbooks.

2. Copy
Prepare for writing with good posture, pencil grip, and use of the helper hand.
Demonstrate 2 again on the Slate Chalkboard, saying the step-by-step directions together.
Children watch, then copy 2's. Next, children copy the bottom row of numbers.

3. Check & Evaluate
Help children ☑ their number for correct Start, Steps, and Bump.
Evaluate the correct formation for numbers 1 and 2.

Read, Color & Draw
Read the label: **two alligators**. Read the sentences: **I can write 2. I can count to 2.**
Encourage free coloring and drawing. Add grass, rocks, etc.

More to Learn
Use the workbook to read/count out loud by 2's. Start on
page 2 and read the left hand page numbers to 10 or more.

Support/ELL
Build 2 on the Mat for Wood Pieces (p. 57).
Start at the ☺. Use 1 Big Curve and 1 Little Line.

CONNECTIONS

Math Link: Create simple AB patterns using 2 objects
or 2 colors. Once children master AB patterns, introduce
ABC patterns.

🔘 **Technology Link:** Use the Digital Teaching Tools
to demonstrate numbers for children to Air Write. Visit
hwtears.com/dtt

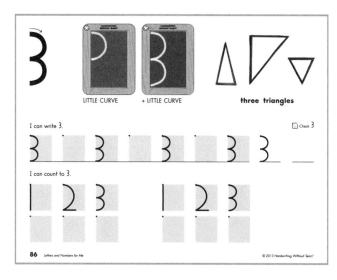

OBJECTIVE: To write number 3 with correct formation.

Lesson Plan
Let's find the number 3 page. Help children turn to p. 86. Discuss what's on the page.
Three starts at the top in the Starting Corner ☺. Have children point to the Starting Corner.

1. **Demonstrate**
   Demonstrate 3 on the Slate Chalkboard, whiteboard, or flip chart.
   Use "My Teacher Writes," track 21, *Rock, Rap, Tap & Learn* CD for 1, 2, and 3.
   Children finger trace the large number 3 in their workbooks.

2. **Copy**
   Prepare for writing with good posture, pencil grip, and use of the helper hand.
   Demonstrate 3 again on the Slate Chalkboard, saying the step-by-step directions together.
   Children watch, then copy 3's. Next, children copy the bottom row of numbers.

3. **Check & Evaluate**
   Help children ☑ their number for correct Start, Steps, and Bump.
   Evaluate the correct formation for numbers 1, 2, and 3.

Read, Color & Draw
Read the label: **three triangles**. Read the sentences: **I can write 3. I can count to 3.**
Encourage free coloring and drawing. Color the triangles different colors.

More to Learn
Use the workbook to read odd numbers. Start on page 1
and read the right hand page numbers to 9 or more.

Support/ELL
Build 3 on the Mat for Wood Pieces (p. 57).
Start at the ☺. Use 2 Little Curves.

CONNECTIONS

Math Link: Introduce the Latin term, "tri," meaning 3.
Show pictures of triangles, tricycles, tridents, tripods,
triplets. Count the corners of the triangles.

LITTLE LINE   + LITTLE LINE   + BIG LINE

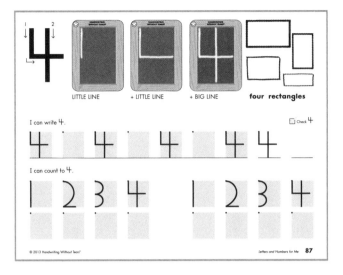

OBJECTIVE: To write number 4 with correct formation.

Lesson Plan
Let's find the number 4 page. Help children turn to p. 87. Discuss what's on the page.
Four starts at the top in the Starting Corner ☺. Have children point to the Starting Corner.

1. **Demonstrate**
   Demonstrate 4 on the Slate Chalkboard, whiteboard, or flip chart.
   Use Wet-Dry-Try on the Slate Chalkboard for 4 (multisensory activity p. 159).
   Children finger trace the large number 4 in their workbooks.

2. **Copy**
   Prepare for writing with good posture, pencil grip, and use of the helper hand.
   Demonstrate 4 again on the Slate Chalkboard, saying the step-by-step directions together.
   Children watch, then copy 4's. Next, children copy the bottom row of numbers.

3. **Check & Evaluate**
   Help children ☑ their number for correct Start, Steps, and Bump.
   Evaluate the correct formation for numbers 1, 2, 3, and 4.

Read, Color & Draw
Read the label: **four rectangles**. Read the sentences: **I can write 4. I can count to 4.**
Encourage free coloring and drawing. Color the rectangles different colors.

More to Learn
Children need to recognize both 4 and 4 as the number four. Talk about reading both, but writing 4.

Support/ELL
Cars and farm animals are excellent for counting to 4. Bring in stuffed animals to make counting to 4 fun. Teach 2 legs in front and 2 in back make 4.

CONNECTIONS

Math Link: Consider reading the book *Rectangles* by Sarah L. Schuette. Show children a Slate Chalkboard. Trace the inside frame to draw a rectangle.

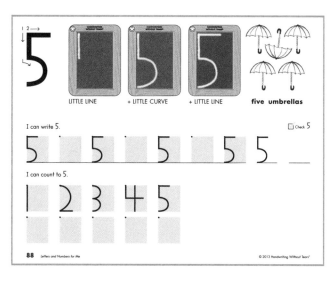

OBJECTIVE: To write number **5** with correct formation.

Lesson Plan

Let's find the number 5 page. Help children turn to p. 88. Discuss what's on the page.
Five starts at the top in the Starting Corner ☺. Have children point to the Starting Corner.

1. Demonstrate

Demonstrate **5** on the Slate Chalkboard, whiteboard, or flip chart.
Use "Number Song," track 20, *Rock, Rap, Tap & Learn* CD.
Children finger trace the large number **5** in their workbooks.

2. Copy

Prepare for writing with good posture, pencil grip, and use of the helper hand.
Demonstrate **5** again on the Slate Chalkboard, saying the step-by-step directions together.
Children watch, then copy **5**'s. Next, children copy the bottom row of numbers.

3. Check & Evaluate

Help children ☑ their number for correct Start, Steps, and Bump.
Evaluate the correct formation for numbers **1**, **2**, **3**, **4**, and **5**.

Read, Color & Draw

Read the label: **five umbrellas**. Read the sentences: **I can write 5. I can count to 5.**
Encourage free coloring and drawing. Add rain drops, puddles, etc.

More to Learn

Trace fingers/hands and count by **5**'s to see how many fingers are in the class.

Support/ELL

Some children come to kindergarten writing **5** in a continuous stroke. We teach two steps to avoid **5** turning into letter **S**.

CONNECTIONS

Science Link: Discuss the **5** senses (sight, smell, hearing, touch, taste) and how they work together.

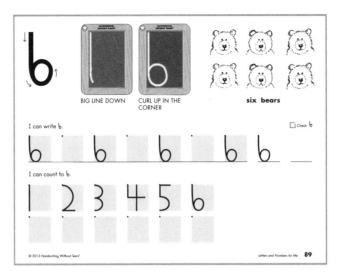

OBJECTIVE: To write number 6 with correct formation.

Lesson Plan
Let's find the number 6 page. Help children turn to p. 89. Discuss what's on the page.
Six starts at the top in the Starting Corner ☺. Have children point to the Starting Corner.

1. Demonstrate
Demonstrate 6 on the Slate Chalkboard, whiteboard, or flip chart.
Use Wet-Dry-Try on the Slate Chalkboard for 6 (multisensory activity p. 159).
Children finger trace the large number 6 in their workbooks.

2. Copy
Prepare for writing with good posture, pencil grip, and use of the helper hand.
Demonstrate 6 again on the Slate Chalkboard, saying the step-by-step directions together.
Children watch, then copy 6's. Next, children copy the bottom row of numbers.

3. Check & Evaluate
Help children ☑ their number for correct Start, Steps, and Bump.
Evaluate the correct formation for numbers 1, 2, 3, 4, 5, and 6.

Read, Color & Draw
Read the label: **six bears**. Read the sentences: **I can write 6. I can count to 6.**
Encourage free coloring and drawing. Add a jar of honey, baby bears, etc.

More to Learn
Show children how to begin 6 with a straight line on the left to avoid reversals. With use, 6 will begin to curve nicely, and won't be reversed.

Support/ELL
Watching you move a highlighter to write 6 for pencil tracing helps children know how to move the pencil. Make sure you are using correct grip and correct steps.

CONNECTIONS

Language Arts Link: Have a reader's theater and read stories about *Goldilocks and the Three Bears*. Discuss how the books are similar and different.

⏻ Technology Link: Use the Digital Teaching Tools to demonstrate numbers for children to Air Write. Visit **hwtears.com/dtt**

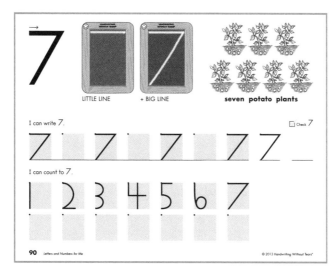

LITTLE LINE   + BIG LINE

seven potato plants

I can write 7.

☐ Check 7

I can count to 7.

1 2 3 4 5 6 7

90 Letters and Numbers for Me   © 2013 Handwriting Without Tears®

OBJECTIVE: To write number **7** with correct formation.

Lesson Plan
Let's find the number 7 page. Help children turn to p. 90. Discuss what's on the page.
Seven starts at the top in the Starting Corner ☺. Have children point to the Starting Corner.

1. **Demonstrate**
   Demonstrate **7** on the Slate Chalkboard, whiteboard, or flip chart.
   Use Door Tracing for **7** (multisensory activity p. 64). Let **7** "walk" across the door top.
   Children finger trace the large number **7** in their workbooks.

2. **Copy**
   Prepare for writing with good posture, pencil grip, and use of the helper hand.
   Demonstrate **7** on the Slate Chalkboard, saying the step-by-step directions together.
   Children watch, then copy **7**'s. Next, children copy the bottom row of numbers.

3. **Check & Evaluate**
   Help children ☑ their number for correct Start, Steps, and Bump.
   Evaluate the correct formation for numbers **1, 2, 3, 4, 5, 6,** and **7**.

Read, Color & Draw
Read the label: **seven potato plants**. Read the sentences: **I can write 7. I can count to 7.**
Encourage free coloring and drawing. Add the sun, blue for the sky, etc.

More to Learn
Read page numbers in the workbook. Sit on child's right.
You read the right page numbers, and child reads left the
page numbers.

Support/ELL
Use a calendar to read numbers up to **7**. Turn to every
month and read to **7** or higher.

CONNECTIONS

Social Studies Link: There are **7** continents in the
world. Show children a globe or a map and teach
children the names of the continents.

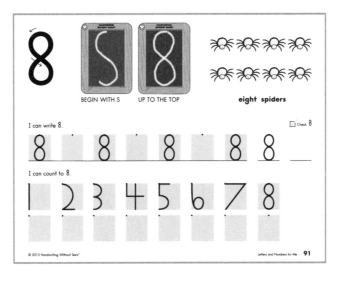

OBJECTIVE: To write number **8** with correct formation.

Lesson Plan
Let's find the number 8 page. Help children turn to p. 91. Discuss what's on the page.
Eight starts at the top center. Have children point to the top center.

1. Demonstrate
Demonstrate **8** on the Slate Chalkboard, whiteboard, or flip chart.
Use Wet-Dry-Try on the Slate Chalkboard for **8** (multisensory activity p. 159).
Children finger trace the large number **8** in their workbooks.

2. Copy
Prepare for writing with good posture, pencil grip, and use of the helper hand.
Demonstrate **8** again on the Slate Chalkboard, saying the step-by-step directions together.
Children watch, then copy **8**'s. Next, children copy the bottom row of numbers.

3. Check & Evaluate
Help children ☑ their number for correct Start, Steps, and Bump.
Evaluate the correct formation for numbers **1, 2, 3, 4, 5, 6, 7,** and **8**.

Read, Color & Draw
Read the label: **eight spiders**. Read the sentences: **I can write 8. I can count to 8.**
Encourage free coloring and drawing. Add a spider web, etc.

More to Learn
Practice changing directions in the stroke to make **8**. Start at the top. Try walking **8**'s around traffic cones. Try racing cars on an **8** track.

Support/ELL
8 requires changing direction. **8** is challenging. Highlight **8**'s for children to pencil trace.

CONNECTIONS

Language Arts Link: Read nursery rhymes "Little Miss Muffett" and "The Itsy Bitsy Spider." Have children discuss what the spider does in each rhyme.

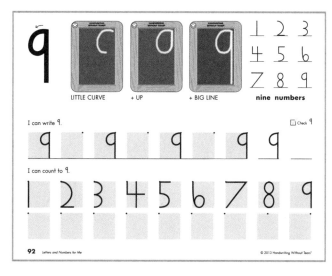

OBJECTIVE: To write number 9 with correct formation.

Lesson Plan
Let's find the number 9 page. Help children turn to p. 92. Discuss what's on the page.
Nine has its own corner. Have children point to the other corner.

1. **Demonstrate**
   Demonstrate 9 on the Slate Chalkboard, whiteboard, or flip chart.
   Use "Number Song," track 20, *Rock, Rap, Tap, & Learn* CD.
   Children finger trace the large number 9 in their workbooks.

2. **Copy**
   Prepare for writing with good posture, pencil grip, and use of the helper hand.
   Demonstrate 9 again on the Slate Chalkboard, saying the step-by-step directions together.
   Children watch, then copy 9's. Next, children copy the bottom row of numbers.

3. **Check & Evaluate**
   Help children ✓ their number for correct Start, Steps, and Bump.
   Evaluate the correct formation for numbers 1, 2, 3, 4, 5, 6, 7, 8, and 9.

Read, Color & Draw
Read the label: **nine numbers.** Read the sentences: **I can write 9. I can count to 9.**

More to Learn
Talk about writing lowercase **a** and number 9. Write **a** on the board (no lines) and change **a** into 9. Lowercase **a** and number 9 start the same!

Support/ELL
9 starts in the top right corner. Make sure the children make 9 in a continuous stroke with the Little Curve to the corner first.

CONNECTIONS

Social Studies Link: Ask children to find the number 9 in the classroom. The calendar is a good place to start. Ask them to explain why numbers repeat on a calendar.

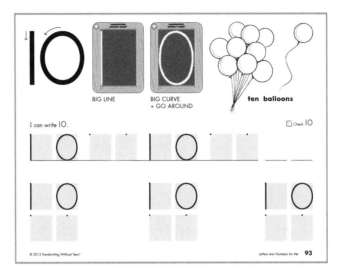

OBJECTIVE: To write number **10** with correct formation.

Lesson Plan
Let's find the number 10 page. Help children turn to p. 93. Discuss what's on the page.

1. Demonstrate
Demonstrate **10** on two Slate Chalkboards, whiteboard, or flip chart.
Use "10 Fingers," track 22, *Rock, Rap, Tap & Learn* CD.
Children finger trace the large number **10** in their workbooks.

2. Copy
Prepare for writing with good posture, pencil grip, and use of the helper hand.
Demonstrate **10** again on the Slate Chalkboards, saying the step-by-step directions together.
Children watch, then copy **10**'s. Next, children copy the bottom row of numbers.

3. Check & Evaluate
Help children ☑ their number for correct Start, Steps, and Bump.
Evaluate the correct formation for number **10**.

Read, Color & Draw
Read the label: **ten balloons**. Read the sentences: **I can write 10. I can count to 10.**
Encourage free coloring and drawing. Color balloons different colors.

More to Learn
10 is the first two-digit number children write. Digit also means finger. Hold up **2** fingers. **10** uses **2** places.

Support/ELL
Body math works! Teach **10** with fingers. Use the hands in your classroom to count by **10**'s.

CONNECTIONS

Math Link: Count by tens. Use fingers, coffee straws, number grids, etc. Show children that ten **1**'s are the same as **10**.

🏠 **Home Link:** This is the end of the numbers. A description of numbers and home practice is available at **hwtears.com/click**

Numbers for Me

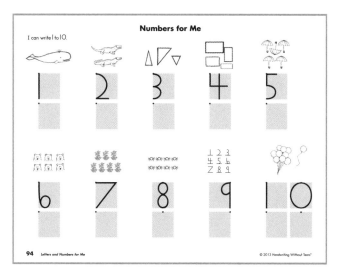

OBJECTIVE: To write all of the numbers with correct formation.

Lesson Plan

Help children turn to p. 94. Read the title. Read the numbers.

1. Demonstrate numbers 1-5 for children to copy.
Gather a Slate Chalkboard, chalk, and eraser.
Prepare for writing with good posture, pencil grip, and use of the helper hand.
Demonstrate each number and wait for children to copy.

2. Demonstrate numbers 6-10 for children to copy.
Prepare for writing with good posture, pencil grip, and use of the helper hand.
Demonstrate each number and wait for children to copy.

3. Check & Evaluate
Check that the numbers are made with correct formation.

More to Learn

There are two rows for rectangles, umbrellas, bears, plants, and spiders. Count the number in each row. If the rows are equal, it's an even number.

Support/ELL

Use a Little Chalk Bit and a Slate Chalkboard to preview numbers individually.

CONNECTIONS

⏻ **Technology Link:** Review numbers 1–10 by using large movements with the Digital Teaching Tools at **hwtears.com/dtt**

RESOURCES

Handwriting Record

Once your students develop good handwriting habits, they'll begin to apply them to their daily work. Download and use this handwriting record to keep track of your students' handwriting progress. Simply observe your students while they are doing daily writing and place a tally mark next to areas of concern. It's helpful to reflect on the information when completing report cards and during family-teacher conferences. It also lets you see who needs additional review or specialized intervention.

Handwriting Record   QTR _____

Student Name	Reversals	Formation	Size	Neatness	Spacing
Sam Smith	///	/			

Notes about pencil grips: _Talk to OT about John and Sadie's grips._ _____
_____
_____

⏻ To gather more detailed information or to monitor your students handwriting progress throughout the year, consider using the Screener of Handwriting Proficiency available at **hwtears.com/screener**

Kindergarten Teaching Guidelines

We're delighted that you're using Handwriting Without Tears® and we want to support you through the year. These guidelines are like a travel guide for the year. We'll suggest activities along the way, but you set the pace. Please think of the guidelines as a sequence, rather than a schedule.

Readiness Activities – The first two weeks of the school year are dedicated to readiness which will prepare children for a year of learning. These delightful, entry-level activities develop school behaviors: saying hello, sharing, passing, talking, taking turns, and following directions. Other activities directly prepare children for handwriting success. Readiness activities help children understand your words. With readiness activities, children learn the words used for letter instruction. They learn how to build letters before they start using their workbooks. You can use Capital Letter Cards for Wood Pieces (p. 56) as a center based activity or Sign In, Please! (p. 41) to start your day. As you get to know your students and the activities, you'll know what's best. Continue readiness activities as you like, throughout the year.

Numbers – Numbers may be at the back of *Letters and Numbers for Me* (p. 83), but they're taught at the beginning of kindergarten. Starting in Week 3, teach two numbers a week during math time. Begin with the Wet-Dry-Try on the Slate Chalkboard activity (p. 159), and then go directly to the workbook lesson page.

Capitals – Every week starts with Monday as a multisensory day. Children have already built capitals with Wood Pieces (readiness activity). Now, they're learning how to write capitals on the Slate Chalkboard with the Wet-Dry-Try activity. This strategy prevents reversals and teaches stroke sequence. We have selected the letters which are the most important to teach on the Slate Chalkboard, but you can use Wet-Dry-Try with any and all letters, if you prefer. If you don't have Slate Chalkboards, do a different favorite activity.

Letters, Words, Sentences & More – Like capitals, every week begins with Monday as a multisensory (no workbook) day. Do Wet-Dry-Try on the Blackboard with Double Lines or another favorite activity of yours.

Favorite activities include:

- Air Writing, p. 61
- Laser Letters, p. 62
- My Teacher Writes, p. 63
- Teaching with Technology, p. 66
- The Hand Activity, p. 104

- Blackboard with Double Lines, p. 105
- Letter Stories, pp. 106–107
- Diver Letters' School, p. 109
- Voices, p. 118
- *Rock, Rap, Tap & Learn* CD, pp. 65, 108

Practice on Double Line Notebook Paper. When you introduce other styles of paper, be sure to model tall, small, and descending letter placement for your students.

Activity Pages – Engaging activities introduce punctuation, capitalization, abbreviations, compound words, rhyming poems, paragraphs, even quotations. These pages are planned after each letter group and after all letters have been taught. Activity pages help give children a wide range of language arts experiences.

 Handwriting All Year (Weeks 23–36) – The workbook ends, but handwriting practice doesn't. We've planned many activities and a routine for maintaining the good habits you carefully taught.

On Mondays you'll focus on capitals, and on Tuesdays you'll work on lowercase letters. Wednesdays are set aside to review words. Thursdays you'll spend time doing sentences, paragraphs, and other language arts activities. Fridays are a day to review numbers and your favorite activities. Visit **hwtears.com/click** to download the Handwriting All Year activities.

Kindergarten Teaching Guidelines

NOTES	WEEK	MONDAY	TUESDAY
	1	**Readiness** Shake Hands with Me, p. 26 Trade, Polish & Sort Wood Pieces, p. 33	**Readiness** Positions & Body Parts, pp. 34–35 *Rock, Rap, Tap & Learn* CD, track 2
	2	**Readiness** Capitals on the Mat, p. 57 for **F, E, D, P, B, R, N, M**	**Readiness** Show Me Magnetic Pieces™, p. 58 **H, K, L U, V, W, X, Y, Z**
	3	**Multisensory** Wet-Dry-Try, p. 59 for **F, D**	**Capital F**, p. 69 Show Me Magnetic Pieces™, p. 58 **Number 1**, p. 161
	4	**Multisensory** Wet-Dry-Try, p. 59 for **B, N**	**Capital B**, p. 73 Capitals on the Door, p. 64 **Number 3**, p. 163
	5	**Multisensory** Wet-Dry-Try, p. 59 for **H, K**	**Capitals** Review Frog Jump Capitals, p. 77 **Number 5**, p. 165
	6	**Multisensory** Wet-Dry-Try, p. 59 for **V, X**	**Capital U**, p. 81 Laser Letters, p. 62 **Number 7**, p. 167
	7	**Multisensory** Wet-Dry-Try, p. 59 for **Z**	**Capital Y**, p. 85 *Rock, Rap, Tap & Learn* CD, track 21 **Number 9**, p. 169
	8	**Multisensory** Wet-Dry-Try, p. 59 for **C, G**	**Capital C**, p. 88 Capitals on the Door, p. 64
	9	**Multisensory** Wet-Dry-Try, p. 59 for **S, A**	**Capitals** Magic C Capitals, p. 92
	10	**Multisensory** Wet-Dry-Try, p. 59 for **T, J**	**Capital T**, p. 96 *Rock, Rap, Tap & Learn* CD, track 14
	11	**Capitals** Capitals for Me **I–Q**, p. 99	**Capitals** Capitals for Me **R–Z**, p. 99
	12	**Favorite Activity** s, v, p. 175	**Lowercase s**, p. 112 Letter Story, p. 107

176 *Kindergarten Teacher's Guide: Resources*   © 2013 Handwriting Without Tears®

Kindergarten Teaching Guidelines

WEDNESDAY	THURSDAY	FRIDAY
Readiness Sign In, Please! p. 41 *Rock, Rap, Tap & Learn* CD, track 9	**Readiness** Curves & Circles, pp. 36–37 Build & Sing Mat Man®, pp. 28–29	**Readiness** Vertical, Horizontal & Diagonal Positions, pp. 38–39 Draw Mat Man®, pp. 30–31
Readiness Capitals on the Mat, p. 57 for **C, O, Q, G**	**Readiness** Show Me Magnetic Pieces™, p. 58 **S, A, I, T, J**	**Evaluate** Screener of Handwriting Proficiency **hwtears.com/screener**
Capital E, p. 70 Show Me Magnetic Pieces™, p. 58	**Capital D**, p. 71 Show Me Magnetic Pieces™, p. 58 **Number 2**, p. 162	**Capital P**, p. 72 Show Me Magnetic Pieces™, p. 58
Capital R, p. 74 Capitals on the Door, p. 64	**Capital N**, p. 75 Capitals on the Door, p. 64 **Number 4**, p. 164	**Capital M**, p. 76 Capitals on the Door, p. 64
Capital H, p. 78 *Rock, Rap, Tap & Learn* CD, track 13	**Capital K**, p. 79 Letter Story, p. 106 **Number 6**, p. 166	**Capital L**, p. 80 Air Writing, p. 61
Capital V, p. 82 *Rock, Rap, Tap & Learn* CD, track 15	**Capital W**, p. 83 *Rock, Rap, Tap & Learn* CD, track 5 **Number 8**, p. 168	**Capital X**, p. 84 Laser Letters, p. 62
Capital Z, p. 86 *Rock, Rap, Tap & Learn* CD, track 15	**Capital Review** Words for Me, p. 87 **Number 10**, p. 170	**Number Review** Numbers for Me, p. 171
Capital O, p. 89 Laser Letters, p. 62	**Capital Q**, p. 90 Laser Letters, p. 62	**Capital G**, p. 91 Laser Letters, p. 62
Capital S, p. 93 *Rock, Rap, Tap & Learn* CD, track 21	**Capital A**, p. 94 *Rock, Rap, Tap & Learn* CD, track 13	**Capital I**, p. 95 *Rock, Rap, Tap & Learn* CD, track 14
Capital J, p. 97 *Rock, Rap, Tap & Learn* CD, track 14	**Capital Review** Words for Me, p. 98	**Capitals** Capitals for Me **A–H**, p. 99
Multisensory *Rock, Rap, Tap & Learn* CD, track 16 Wet-Dry-Try, p. 105 for **c, o**	**Lowercase c**, p. 110 *Rock, Rap, Tap & Learn* CD, track 16	**Lowercase o**, p. 111 The Hand Activity, p. 104
Words s words, p. 113	**Lowercase v**, p. 114 *Rock, Rap, Tap & Learn* CD, track 15	**Lowercase w**, p. 115 *Rock, Rap, Tap & Learn* CD, track 15

Kindergarten Teaching Guidelines

NOTES	WEEK	MONDAY	TUESDAY
	13	**Favorite Activity** **a**, **d**, p. 175	**Lowercase t**, p. 116 Letter Story, p. 107
	14	**Favorite Activity** **g**, **u**, p. 175	**Lowercase g**, p. 121 Letter Story, p. 106
	15	**Favorite Activity** **e**, p. 175	**Lowercase i**, p. 126 *Rock, Rap, Tap & Learn* CD, track 11
	16	**Favorite Activity** **k**, **y**, p. 175	**Lowercase k**, p. 130 Letter Story, p. 106
	17	**Favorite Activity** **p**, **r**, p. 175	**Lowercase p**, p. 134 *Rock, Rap, Tap & Learn* CD, track 18
	18	**Favorite Activity** **h**, **b**, p. 175	**Lowercase m**, p. 138 Letter Story, p. 107
	19	**Favorite Activity** **f**, **q**, p. 175	**Lowercase f**, p. 142 Letter Story, p. 106
	20	**Favorite Activity** **z**, p. 175	**Lowercase z**, p. 146 Letter Story, p. 107
	21	**Favorite Activity** Sentence Song, p. 122	**Language Arts Activities** **Sentences** Punctuation (top half), p. 150
	22	**Favorite Activity** Sentence Song, p. 122	**Language Arts Activities** **Poem** A Spider, p. 153
	23	**Capitals** Missing Letters	**Lowercase Letters** Magic c Letters: **c**, **o**, **a**, **d**, **g**
	24	**Capitals** Write Road, Safety & Information Signs	**Lowercase Letters** Diver Letters: **p**, **r**, **n**, **m**, **h**, **b**

Kindergarten Teaching Guidelines

WEDNESDAY	THURSDAY	FRIDAY
Lowercase Review Words for Me, p. 117	**Lowercase a**, p. 119 Voices, p. 118	**Lowercase d**, p. 120 Voices, p. 118
Lowercase Review Sentences for Me, p. 123	**Lowercase u**, p. 124 *Rock, Rap, Tap & Learn* CD, track 11	**Lowercase Review** Words & Sentence for Me, p. 125
Lowercase e, p. 127 Letter Story, p. 106	**Lowercase l**, p. 128 Air Writing, p. 61	**Lowercase Review** Words & Sentence for Me, p. 129
Lowercase Review Words & Sentence for Me, p. 131	**Lowercase y**, p. 132 *Rock, Rap, Tap & Learn* CD, track 15	**Lowercase j**, p. 133 *Rock, Rap, Tap & Learn* CD, track 19
Lowercase Review Words & Sentence for Me, p. 135	**Lowercase r**, p. 136 *Rock, Rap, Tap & Learn* CD, track 18	**Lowercase n**, p. 137 Air Writing, p. 61
Lowercase Review Words & Sentence for Me, p. 139	**Lowercase h**, p. 140 *Rock, Rap, Tap & Learn* CD, track 18	**Lowercase b**, p. 141 Letter Story, p. 106
Lowercase Review Words & Sentence for Me, p. 143	**Lowercase q**, p. 144 Letter Story, p. 107	**Lowercase x**, p. 145 *Rock, Rap, Tap & Learn* CD, track 15
Lowercase Review Words & Sentence for Me, p. 147	**Language Arts Activities** **Letters** Magic c Mystery Letters, p. 148	**Language Arts Activities** **Words** Labels, p. 149
Language Arts Activities **Sentences** Punctuation (bottom half), p. 150	**Language Arts Activities** **Paragraph** Fire Drill, p. 151	**Language Arts Activities** **Words** Rhymes, p. 152
Language Arts Activities **Sentences** Greetings, p. 154	**Language Arts Activities** More Sentences, p. 155	**Evaluate** Screener of Handwriting Proficiency **hwtears.com/screener**
Words Printing Letters in a Word	**Sentences & More** Watch the Teacher & Write	**Numbers** Wet-Dry-Try, p. 159 **Favorite Activity**, p. 175
Words Sick Word Clinic	**Sentences & More** Sentence Spacing with Pennies	**Numbers** Numbers l–l0, pp. 161–170 **Favorite Activity**, p. 175

Kindergarten Teaching Guidelines

NOTES	WEEK	MONDAY	TUESDAY
	25	**Capitals** Play the Mystery Letter Game for Frog Jump Capitals	**Lowercase Letters** Same as Capitals **c, o, s, v, w, x, z**
	26	**Capitals** Review **F, E, D, P, B, R, N, M**	**Lowercase Letters** Missing Letters
	27	**Capitals** Review Diagonal Capitals **A, K, M, N, V, W** with States	**Lowercase Letters** Where Do You Start Your Letters? At the Top!
	28	**Capitals** An Alphabetical Roll Call	**Lowercase Letters** Review **e, o, a, t, n, s**
	29	**Capitals** A Capital Search	**Lowercase Letters** Teach **T & t**
	30	**Capitals** Sign In, Please!	**Lowercase Letters** Envelope Words with Two Letters
	31	**Capitals** Teaching Initials	**Lowercase Letters** Envelope Words with Three Letters
	32	**Capitals** Make a Compass Rose with **N, S, E, W**	**Lowercase Letters** e Search
	33	**Capitals** Sounds & Capitals	**Lowercase Letters** Names Together
	34	**Capitals** Mystery Letter Game for Sounds	**Lowercase Letters** Descending Letter Teams with Wall Cards
	35	**Capitals** Beginning, Middle & End of the Alphabet	**Lowercase Letters** What's the Match?
	36	**Capitals** What's the Match?	**Lowercase Letters** Lowercase Letter Hunt

Kindergarten Teaching Guidelines

WEDNESDAY	THURSDAY	FRIDAY
Words Magic c Word Review	**Sentences & More** Sick Sentence Clinic	**Numbers** Door Tracing, p. 64 **Favorite Activity**, p. 175
Words Words with Diver Letters **p, r, n, m, h, b**	**Sentences & More** Alliterative Sentence Build	**Numbers** Phone Number/Address **Favorite Activity**, p. 175
Words Match Pictures to Words	**Sentences & More** Punctuation Practice	**Numbers** Calendar **Favorite Activity**, p. 175
Words Birthday Names	**Sentences & More** Extra! Extra! Write All About It!	**Numbers** Count & Write **Favorite Activity**, p. 175
Words Frequently Used Words	**Sentences & More** Sentence Song	**Numbers** Hop Scotch Numbers **Favorite Activity**, p. 175
Words Words with **q**	**Sentences & More** Writer's Workshop	**Numbers** Number Cards **Favorite Activity**, p. 175
Words Word Endings	**Sentences & More** Picture Book Sentences	**Numbers** Play Pyramid **Favorite Activity**, p. 175
Words List of Rhymes	**Sentences & More** Action Sentences	**Numbers** What's Missing? **Favorite Activity**, p. 175
Words Substitute the Letter	**Sentences & More** Question Marks	**Numbers** Missing Numbers **Favorite Activity**, p. 175
Words Leaves & Trees	**Sentences & More** Exclamation Points	**Numbers** More or Less? **Favorite Activity**, p. 175
Words Big Water Words	**Sentences & More** Journal Time	**Numbers** Mystery Numbers **Favorite Activity**, p. 175
Words Word Wall Words	**Sentences & More** Read & Connect	**Numbers** Counting Pennies **Favorite Activity**, p. 175

Rock, Rap, Tap & Learn CD

Rock, Rap, Tap & Learn CD is loaded with upbeat songs to make handwriting fun. The best thing about music is that it promotes movement. Whether you are teaching descending letters or spacing skills, this CD has all you need to charge up your lessons and catch your students' attention. The lyrics are printed inside the jacket cover of the CD.

A Great Addition to the Classroom

The songs tie into activities in the *Kindergarten Teacher's Guide.* They introduce or reinforce concepts being taught to help children practice a given skill. For example, "Where Do You Start Your Letters?" teaches children the terms "top," "middle," and "bottom" while chidren learn that letters start at the top. Other songs help children develop correct formation of letters by having them Air Write along with the lyrics. Children will learn pencil grip, stroke awareness, and spatial concepts, as well as develop improved social-emotional skills and cooperative participation. Adding music and movment to your handwriting lessons not only reinforces concepts, it makes learning and teaching fun!

The best way to use the CD is to first listen to the songs and read the lyrics on your own. Then, play the CD in the background during free play to subtly introduce it to the children. See which songs catch the attention of both you and the children. Think about how the skills fit in with your plans. Here are some ideas to help you along.

Track & Song	Suggested Activities
1 Alphabet Boogie	Have your students do a simple boogie to the ABC's.
2 Where Do You Start Your Letters?	Play a question and answer game with students.
3 Air Writing	Choose a letter and trace it in the air for your class.
4 Hey, Hey! Big Line	Use Wood Pieces Set for Capital Letters to review positional concepts. All you need are the Big Lines.
5 Diagonals	Help children learn the diagonal stroke with ease by writing it in the air.
6 Big Line March	March around with Big Lines for a fun time.
7 Sentence Song	Model a sentence (no more than three words) on the board. Point to: capital, words, spaces, and ending punctuation as children sing.
8 My Bonnie Lies over the Ocean	Have your students sit or stand every time they hear a word starting with **b**.
9 Picking Up My Pencil	Help students learn proper pencil grip with this entertaining exercise (p. 47).
10 Stomp Your Feet	Learn proper pencil grip and posture (p. 43).
11 Vowels	Review the vowels and teach the difference between capital and lowercase.
12 Frog Jump Letters	Children stand up and finger trace the Frog Jump Capitals in the air.
13 Give It A Middle	Help children learn the middle stroke of **A**, **G**, and **H**.
14 Give It A Top	Help children learn the top stroke of **T**, **J**, **I**, and **T**.
15 Sliding Down to the End of the Alphabet	Start with **V** and slide all the way down to **Z**.
16 CAPITALS & lowercase	Teach letters **Cc**, **Oo**, **Ss**, **Vv**, and **Ww** (easy capital/lowercase partners).
17 Magic C Rap	Learn how to use the c stroke to make **a**, **d**, **g**, **o**, and **q** with this memorable rap.
18 Diver Letters' School	Incorporate movement to teach the Diver Letters **p**, **r**, **n**, **m**, **h**, and **b** (p. 109).
19 Descending Letters	Remember lowercase **g**, **j**, **y**, **p**, and **q** with this fun song.
20 Number Song	Write numbers on paper or in the air as you review number formation.
21 My Teacher Writes	Teach your students numbers or letters with this interactive song.
22 10 Fingers	Count by tens. Five children line up side by side. Hold fingers in the air.
23 Mat Man Rock	Use this song to review body parts and to celebrate Mat Man®.
24 Head & Shoulders, Baby!	Use this song in the morning as a warm up or to review body parts.
25 Tapping to the ABC's	Use Wood Pieces Set for Capital Letters to tap out the alphabet.

For a printable list of tracks and suggested activities, visit **hwtears.com/click**

Remediation Tips

General Remediation Tips

Remediation strategies can help you correct handwriting difficulties. In addition, families often ask about ways they can assist their child. This section gives you remediation tips and information for both you and families.

When facilitating handwriting remediation, remember the following:

Notice What's Correct
Recognition of what the student completed correctly is encouraging and should come before any suggestions or corrections. You can give an easy handwriting check called "Check Your Teaching" to your students to see if they learned what you taught. Use it after teaching each letter group, or give it to students to see what they already know and what they need. The check is available for download at **hwtears.com/click**

 Download "Check My Teaching" from A Click Away. Make sure you mark each letter with numbers and arrows to show how it was made. You may spell the words for children.

Keep Practice Short
Ten or fifteen minutes is long enough. You want the child's full attention and optimum effort during the lesson. Then end the lesson while it's still going well or the minute you've lost the child's interest.

Use Imitation
With imitation, the child has the opportunity to see the actual movements that make the letter. Then the child can associate the letter with the movement that produced it. We are as concerned with how a letter is formed as we are with how the end product looks. Imitation has two advantages. It gives the child the best chance to write the letter, and it teaches the correct motor habits.

Communicate
Share strategies with others. If you want to help a child with handwriting, the best thing you can do is to get everyone on the same page. As long as everyone knows what is needed, you can move the remediation along. Some report cards don't have a place to grade or mark handwriting. This is particularly important in the lower grades because handwriting performance can affect other academic subjects.

 If your report card doesn't allow space for handwriting, download this additional form and include it with your students' report cards.

Consistency & Follow-Through
Identify problems, set up the team, and let the progress begin. If you are consistent, you will see progress in the child's handwriting.

Help Others
You may develop a love for helping children with handwriting. With Handwriting Without Tears® training and the HWT program, you can become HWT Level 1 Certified to teach and remediate handwriting. Visit **hwtcertification.com**

Handedness

By the time formal handwriting training begins, it's important for a child to have developed hand dominance. Sometimes you have to help the child choose the more skilled hand and then facilitate the use of that hand. Collaborate with families, teachers, therapists, and other significant individuals in the child's life to determine the more skilled hand. Create a checklist of activities for everyone to observe (brushing teeth, eating, dressing, cutting, etc.). Together, you can position materials on the preferred side and encourage use of the more skilled hand for handwriting. If both hands are equally skilled, choose the right hand.

Pencil Grip

Always demonstrate the correct grip and finger positions. Use the Picking Up My Pencil activity on p. 47 in this teacher's guide and sing "Picking Up My Pencil," track 9, *Rock, Rap, Tap & Learn* CD.

Correct Pencil Grip in Three Easy Steps

You can help a child develop a correct pencil grip or fix a grip that is awkward. Teach grip in three stages, and you will be impressed with how easy it becomes. The technique needs consistency and a little time (see p. 46 for an illustration of correct grips). Explain to students that you are going to show them a new way to hold their pencil, but that they are not yet allowed to use the new grip for their writing.

1. Pick-Up—Have children pick up their pencils and hold it in the air with their fingers and thumb correctly placed. Help position the fingers, if necessary. Say, "Wow, that is a perfect pencil grip. Now make a few circles in the air with the perfect pencil grip. Drop it and do it again." Repeat this five times a day for a couple of weeks.

2. Scribble & Wiggle with Pencil Pick-Ups—Download and give children the "Pencil Pick-Ups" worksheet. Have them pick up the pencil, hold it correctly, and put the pencil on an image. The little finger side of the pencil hand rests on the paper. Children make wiggly marks, lines, and simple scribbles in the drawings. The helper hand is flat and holds the paper. The advantage of this step is that children develop their pencil grip and finger control without worrying about how the writing looks. Do this daily for a couple weeks.

3. Write—Have children pick up the pencil, hold it correctly, and write the first letter of their names. Add letters until children write their names easily with the correct grip. Once they are writing letters with their new grip, grant them permission to use it for all their writing.

Adaptive Devices

If a child continues to have difficulty holding the pencil, there are a variety of grips available at school supply stores, art/stationery stores, and catalogs. Their usefulness varies from grip to grip and child to child. Experiment with the devices and use them only if they make it easier for the child to hold the pencil correctly. With young children, physical devices should not be used as a substitute for physical demonstration.

Remediation Tips

Rubber Band Trick

Check the angle of the pencil. If it's pointing straight up, the pencil will be difficult to hold and will cause tension in the fingertips. Put a rubber band around the child's wrist. Loop another rubber band to the first one. Pull the loop over the pencil eraser. This may keep the pencil pulled back at the correct angle. You may make or buy a more comfortable version that uses ponytail holders.

Reward Good Grip

Sometimes young children need motivation to use their new grip. Offer them a small reward for remembering how to hold their pencils correctly. Track their progress so they can see how close they are to reaching their reward. Attach a photo of their correct pencil grip with a small strip of paper to their desks and stamp them every time you catch them holding their pencil correctly.

Check My Grip   Look at me, I'm holding my pencil correctly.

① ② ③ ④ ⑤
⑥ ⑦ ⑧ ⑨ ⑩

My reward is:

Pencil Pressure

Sometimes children have to learn to judge and moderate their pencil pressure. It's more common for a child to push too hard than not hard enough. Regardless, both can cause problems.

Too Hard: Try a mechanical pencil so the child has to control the amount of pressure. You can also have children place the paper on a mouse pad (if they press too hard, they will poke holes in their paper).*

Too Soft: Have the child pencil in small shapes until they are black. Use pencils with softer lead.

*Suggestions should be tried at home before they're used at school, because remedies for pencil pressure problems can be frustrating to the child.

Helper Hand

We've all seen helper hands in laps, twirling hair, or propping up foreheads. You can nag the child, but you'll get better results if you talk directly to the hand! Take the child's helper hand in yours and pretend to talk to that hand.

Name the helper hand. For example, ask John what other name he likes that starts with **J**. If John says "Jeremy," tell him that you are going to name his helper hand "Jeremy." Have a little talk with Jeremy, the helper hand. Tell Jeremy that he's supposed to help by holding the paper. Say that John is working really hard on his handwriting, but he needs Jeremy's help. Show Jeremy where he's supposed to be. Tell John that he might have to remind Jeremy about his job.

Children find this very funny. They don't get embarrassed because it's the helper hand, not the child who is being corrected. It's not John who needs to improve, it's Jeremy. This is a face-saving, but effective, reminder. A flat (but not stiff) helper hand promotes relaxed writing. Put your hand flat on the table and try to feel tension—there isn't any. Make a fist and feel the tension! Children can get uptight while writing, but a flat helper hand decreases tension.

The Eraser Challenge

Some children spend a lot of time erasing. Those who erase often will tend to be slow and lag behind in their work. If you want to control the amount of erasing without taking away erasers, compromise with the following strategy:

1. Download The Eraser Challenge.
2. Tape them to children's desks or send them home for families to use when helping with homework.
3. Every time children erase, they pull a flag.
4. Play a game by challenging children to have a certain amount of flags left at the end of the day.

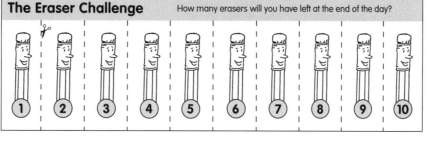

The Eraser Challenge How many erasers will you have left at the end of the day?

My Handwriting Checklist

Some children have good handwriting skills but don't carry them over into general school work. Make your expectations clear and make children accountable. Download and print notes to help children evaluate their work before they turn it in.

Spacing

Teach your students to put letters in a word close to each other. Have them put their index fingers up and bring them close together, without touching. Say, "In a word, the letters are close, but don't touch." Draw fingers for them on their paper as a reminder.

Sick Sentence Clinic

Write a sentence with the letters too far apart. Circle each word in the sentence. Now, copy the sentence over, putting the letters closer. For example:

> I a m b i g.   I am   big.

Now, write a sentence with the letters too close. Children underline each word in the sentence. Now, copy the sentence over with spaces between the words.

> Icanrun.   I can run.

The Nothing Bottle

If students run their words together: Say that you will give them what they need to create spaces. Have them hold out their hands to catch it. Take a huge empty bottle (or any container) and make a big show of pouring into their hands. Ask, "What did you get?" Nothing! Tell them to put nothing after every word they write.

Making a Magic C Bunny

The Magic C Bunny helps you teach c-based lowercase letters **o**, **a**, **d**, **g**, and **q**. The Magic C Bunny Puppet will bring your lessons to life.

What Does the Magic C Bunny Do?
- He changes letter **c** into new letters. That's his magic trick.
- He plays Mystery Letter (p. 148) and Voices game (p. 118).
- He makes learning fun.
- He creates a good Magic c habit for **a**, **d**, **g**, **o**, and even **q**.

Multisensory Activities
Have fun with the "Magic C Rap," track 17, *Rock, Rap, Tap & Learn* CD. This song is a great way to get your students engaged and excited about Magic c Letters.

- Introduce Magic C Bunny while playing the "Magic C Rap."
- Teach children to sing the chorus:

> Magic **c**, **c** for **a d** and **g**
> Magic **c**, **c** for **a d** and **g**
> Magic **c**, **c** for **a d** and **g**
> And before you're through, do **o** and **q**

- Introduce the song before demonstrating Magic c Letters on the board. Use the Voices activity and have Magic C Bunny whisper which voices your class should use into your ear.

Make the Magic C Bunny

1 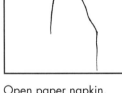	**2**	**3** 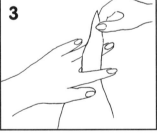	**4** 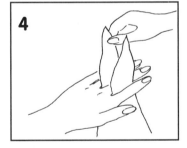
Open paper napkin. Hold by one corner.	Spread index and middle fingers apart.	Pull corner between your index and middle fingers. (First ear)	Take the next corner. Pull corner between your middle and ring fingers. (Second ear)

5 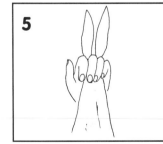	**6** 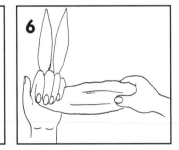	**7** 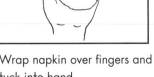	**8** 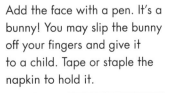
Fold fingers into palm.	Pull napkin out to side.	Wrap napkin over fingers and tuck into hand.	Add the face with a pen. It's a bunny! You may slip the bunny off your fingers and give it to a child. Tape or staple the napkin to hold it.

Sentence School®

The Sentence School program works alongside the Handwriting Without Tears® handwriting curriculum to teach the skills kindergarten children need to build sentences and become confident, skillful writers. Although *Sentence School* is not included in our teaching guidelines, you may want to add it as a language arts activity for Mondays, Wednesdays, and Fridays.

The Sentence School Curriculum

Supports your teaching:

- Integrates with your existing curricula
- Engages students and reinforces concepts through movement, touch, sight, and sound
- Fits into your language arts time block
- Takes only 10–15 minutes a day

Children will:

- Increase vocabulary—learn words and their meanings, and use words in sentences
- Develop conceptual understanding—understand the relationship among words and reinforce their meanings
- Build grammar skills—speak in complete sentences and learn correct grammar through example and practice
- Cultivate writing skills—follow the basic rules: begin with a capital, leave space between words, and end with punctuation

For more information about *Sentence School* and to download a sample lesson visit **hwtears.com**

Monday – Action Sentences

Wednesday – Describing Sentences

Friday – Question and Answers

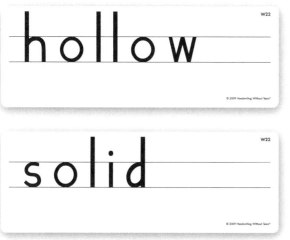

School-to-Home Connections

Research consistently shows that a strong school-to-home connection helps children build self esteem, curiosity, and motivation to learn new things. Home and school are the two most important places for young children. When teachers and families work together, everyone wins. Here are 10 ways to make a strong school-to-home connection:

1. Find opportunities to communicate during planned school events like family-teacher meetings, conferences, and school visits. Take a few extra steps to communicate through letters, email, and even podcasts. Download our "Kindergarten Welcome Letter" from **hwtears.com/click**

2. Share important assessment information about your students' progress. Consider using our Screener of Handwriting Proficiency to monitor progress throughout the year.

3. Share this curriculum with families. Let them play with some of our hands-on products. Tell them about our website, **hwtears.com**, so that they can explore the many resources available.

4. Share music with families. Send children home singing songs from our *Rock, Rap, Tap & Learn* CD. If there is a fun song that families sing at home, ask them to share it with you.

5. Model language and thinking skills out loud. Children benefit from hearing adults talk and solve problems. Send home letter charts so families can use the same language you use in school when talking about letters.

6. Encourage families to read to children as much as possible and to look for letters in the books. Reading is fun and helps build comprehension and language skills. Hunting for letters builds alphabet knowledge.

7. Share the *Letters and Numbers for Me* workbook with families. Send it home when children have completed it. Encourage families to review it with their children and share it with other family members.

8. Help families prepare children to write. Encourage them to learn proper grip and encourage their children to hold a pencil correctly. Teach families how to help children write their names (see next page). These educational articles, along with others, are available for download at **hwtears.com/click**

9. Encourage families to help their children to recognize letters and notice letters all around them. Point out signs, logos, and letters wherever you go.

10. Reinforce learning at home. We have developed A Click Away and Home Links so you can share important handwriting information along the way. Home Links occur after every letter group and help to educate families about handwriting, while providing an opportunity to practice letter formations correctly at home. The icon below is featured throughout this teacher's guide. It will remind you when it's time to send something home.

> 🏠 **Home Link:** This is the end of the first letter group **c, o, s, v, w,** and **t.** A description of these letters and home practice is available at **hwtears.com/click**

Help Me Write My Name

Children love their names! Do your students recognize their names? Do you see them trying to write their names? Teaching children to write their name depends on two things: age and readiness.

To teach developmentally in Pre-K, we suggest you first teach children to write their name in capitals. Then, transition to writing their name in title case at the end of Pre-K or start of kindergarten when children are ready.

Start of Kindergarten: Capital Name

Students won't always write in capitals, but it's the easiest way for them to start. This is especially true for your struggling writers or students with special needs. You can explain that there are two ways to write a name. The big letter way and the little letter way. Show them both, but focus on capitals first. Explain to them that when their hands get stronger, they can learn the other way, too.

1. Teach name in capitals with careful demonstration and imitation activities.

2. Put your strip above the child's strip. Demonstrate each letter on your strip and wait for the child to imitate you. Do this letter by letter (see below).

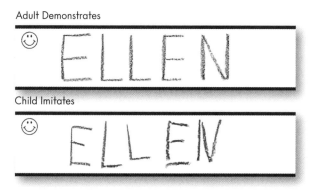

Kindergarten: Title Case Name

When you feel students have had sufficient practice with their capital letters, it's time to add lowercase. Most children look forward to learning this new skill. Teach title case name by using Wet-Dry-Try on the Blackboard with Double Lines (p. 105). This activity allows you to model the letters correctly using a multisensory activity. Consider using this activity as a center based activity for name practice. After practing on the board, have children write their names on a piece of double line paper. You may also repeat the above activity when teaching children their name in title case.

Teaching children their names is a great activity to send home to families. Visit **hwtears.com** to download activities that families can use to help with their name at home.

Handwriting Standards for Kindergarten

Handwriting instruction must adhere to developmental principles to ensure success for all children. Yet, educational guidelines often are limited to one standard in the English Language Arts standards— "produces legible handwriting." When students fail to meet this standard, teachers have no means for examining which skills are lacking.

Handwriting is an essential skill for both children and adults (Feder and Majnemer 2007). Even in the age of technology, handwriting remains the primary tool of communication and knowledge assessment for students in the classroom. The demands for handwriting are great, whether in the classroom or beyond. A 1992 study (McHale and Cermak) found that 85 percent of all fine motor time in second-, fourth- and sixth-grade classrooms was spent on paper and pencil activities. A more recent study (Marr, Cermak, Cohn and Henderson 2003) noted that kindergarten children are now spending 42 percent of their fine motor time on paper and pencil activities. The addition of handwritten components to many state standardized assessments and of a handwritten essay to the College Board SAT further emphasize the importance of handwriting. Furthermore, good handwriting is important long after graduation. In *Script and Scribble* (2009), Florey writes in reference to handwritten job applications, "Like it or not, even in our machine-driven world, people still judge you by your handwriting."

Research literature extensively documents the consequences of poor handwriting on early literacy and academic performance. Children who experience difficulty mastering this skill [handwriting] may avoid writing and decide they cannot write, leading to arrested writing development (Graham, Harris and Fink 2000). Handwriting is critical to the production of creative and well-written text (Graham and Harris 2005) affecting both fluency and the quality of the composition. Handwriting instruction must adhere to developmental principles to ensure success for all children. According to the National Association for the Education of Young Children, newborn to eight-year-old children learn best from methods that are consistent with developmentally appropriate practice (1998). However, due to a general lack of professional development in the area of handwriting, educators are not always aware of the specific objectives to be addressed at various age and grade levels.

Seeing the need for a more specific analysis of skills, a team of occupational therapists and educators developed a set of handwriting standards. We hope it serves as an example to educators and curriculum decision-makers and brings increased attention to this crucial, yet often overlooked, area of education.

Readiness Skills
K.1 Concept Development
Students will demonstrate emergent literacy skills needed for writing. Each student will:
  A. Identify basic shapes (e.g., squares, circles, and triangles)
  B. Recognize simple size differences (e.g., big and little)
  C. Understand position words (e.g., top/bottom, front/back, up/down, in/out)
  D. Demonstrate print awareness
    1. Position a book or page correctly for coloring, writing, or reading
    2. Track pictures, symbols, or letters from top to bottom and left to right
    3. Understand that printed words represent spoken words
  E. Identify printed symbols used for communication
    1. Identify capital letters
    2. Identify lowercase letters
    3. Identify numbers

F. Use drawings and symbols to convey meaning and share ideas
   1. Draw simple shapes (e.g., squares, circles, and triangles)
   2. Draw a person
   3. Use letters to approximate words

K.2 Physical Development
Students will demonstrate physical development needed for writing. Each student will:
   A. Use a correct and efficient pencil grip for writing
   B. Stabilize paper with the non-writing hand while drawing/writing
   C. Position writing paper appropriately
   D. Maintain sitting posture for writing/coloring/drawing

Printing Skills
K.3 Letter Skills
Students will demonstrate skills in printing letters and numbers from memory. Each student will:
   A. Demonstrate correct formation of letters and numbers
      1. Start capital letters at the top
      2. Start numbers at the top
      3. Start lowercase letters (except **d** and **e**) at the top
      4. Follow standard formation sequence for letters and numbers
   B. Orient letters and numbers correctly (with few reversals)
   C. Place letters and numbers on a base line (within 1/8" above or below)
   D. Write letters and numbers in a grade-appropriate size
   E. Follow the writing guidelines of various styles of paper (triple, double, and single lines)

K.4 Word Skills
Students will write letters together to form words. Each student will:
   A. Write his/her name
      1. Begin with a capital letter
      2. Form each letter in a name, moving left to right
   B. Write two- to five-letter words
      1. Form each letter in a word, moving left to right
      2. Use appropriate spacing (i.e., letters close together, NOT touching or overlapping)

K.5 Sentence Skills
Students write words to express thoughts and form sentences. Each student will:
   A. Write simple two- to three-word sentences
   B. Write horizontally, from left to right
   C. Use sentence writing conventions:
      1. Start sentences with a capital letter
      2. Leave a clearly defined space between words
      3. Use ending punctuation
         a. Use a period to end statements
         b. Use a question mark to end questions
         c. Use an exclamation point to end exclamations

Common Core State Standards

What Are They?

The Common Core State Standards were developed in collaboration with teachers, school administrators, and experts in order to provide a clear and consistent framework to prepare all children for college and the workforce. The standards provide consistent, appropriate benchmarks for all students, in the United States. The belief is that the standards will enable students to succeed in entry-level, credit-bearing academic college courses and workforce training programs (NGA 2010). Standards were developed for both English Language Arts and Mathematics. K–12 grade-specific standards are set within each content area.

In the Language Arts standards, there are specific strands for reading, writing, speaking and listening, and language. All of the standards are evidence based and align with overall college and work expectations. While the standards describe specific expectations, each standard does not need to be a separate focus for instruction and assessment. The standards do not describe all that can or should be taught, nor do they define specifically how teachers should teach the standards. Intervention methods or materials necessary to support students who are below or above grade-level expectations are also not included. A great deal is left to the discretion of teachers and curriculum developers (NGA 2010).

How Does Handwriting Without Tears® Align with Common Core State Standards?

We know that handwriting is an important part of a child's language and literacy development. Therefore, the majority of our products and resources correlate best with the English Language Arts standards for Common Core despite there being few specific handwriting standards. Our products and resources meet the goals of multiple standards. Often, a variety of activities and products will achieve the same goal or standard, making it easy to reach children's various learning styles.

The Common Core State Standards are great because they inform what is critical to college and career readiness for children. However, they do not define the readiness skills necessary for children to succeed. Students require a wide range of academic preparation, particularly in early grades. Attention to such matters as social-emotional and physical development are just as important. Our activities and resources develop and build on these necessary skills, which helps to supplement the Common Core State Standards and their pursuit for preparing children for the future.

 For more information about how Handwriting Without Tears curriculum correlates to the Common Core State Standards, visit **hwtears.com/click**

Boyd, Judi, W. Steven Barnett, Elena Bordova, Deborah J. Leong, and Deanna Gomby. 2005. "Promoting Children's Social and Emotional Development Through Preschool Education." New Brunswick, NJ: National Institute for Early Education Research.

Dennis, Julie L., and Yvonne Swinth. 2001. "Pencil Grasp and Children's Handwriting Legibility During Different-Length Writing Tasks." *American Journal of Occupational Therapy* 55 (2): 175–183.

Dolch, Edward William. 1948. *Problems in Reading*. Champaign, IL: The Garrard Press.

Feder, Katya P., and Annette Majnemer. 2007. "Handwriting Development, Competency, and Intervention." *Developmental Medicine & Child Neurology* 49: 312–317.

Florey, Kitty Burns. 2009. *Script and Scribble: The Rise and Fall of Handwriting*. New York: Melville House.

Florida International University. 2012. "Good Handwriting and Good Grades: FIU Researcher Finds New Link." *FIU News*, January 18. http://news.fiu.edu/2012/01/good-handwriting-and-good-grades-fiu-researcher-finds-new-link/34934.

Gesell, Arnold. 1940. *The First Five Years of Life: A Guide to the Study of the Preschool Child*. New York: Harper and Brothers.

Graham, Steve, and Karen R. Harris. 2005. "Improving the Writing Performance of Young Struggling Writers: Theoretical and Programmatic Research from the Center on Accelerating Student Learning." *Journal of Special Education* 39 (10): 19–33.

Graham, Steve, Karen R. Harris, and Barbara Fink. 2000. "Is handwriting causally related to learning to write? Treatment of handwriting problems in beginning writers." *Journal of Educational Psychology* 92: 620–633.

Knapton, Emily. 2011. "Exploring the Levels of Emergent Literacy." *Indiana Reading Journal* 43 (2): 16–18.

Lust, Carol A., and Denise K. Donica. 2011. "Effectiveness of a Handwriting Readiness Program in Head Start: A Two-Group Controlled Trial." *American Journal of Occupational Therapy* 65 (5): 560–568.

Marr, Deborah, Sharon A. Cermack, Ellen S. Cohn, and Anne Henderson. 2003. "Fine Motor Activities in Head Start and Kindergarten Classrooms." *American Journal of Occupational Therapy* 57 (5): 550–557.

McHale, Kathleen, and Sharon Cermak. 1992. "Fine Motor Activities in Elementary School: Preliminary Findings and Provisional Implications for Children with Fine Motor Problems." *American Journal of Occupational Therapy* 46, 10: 898–903.

National Association for the Education of Young Children & International Reading Association. 1998. "Learning to Read and Write: Developmentally Appropriate Practices for Young Children." *Young Children* 53 (4): 30–46. http://www.naeyc.org/files/naeyc/file/positions/PSREAD98.pdf.

National Governors Association Center for Best Practices and Council of Chief State School Officers. 2010. *Common Core State Standards*. Washington, D.C.: National Governors Association Center for Best Practices, Council of Chief State School Officers. www.corestandards.org.

Sousa, David. 2011. *How the Brain Learns*, 4th ed. Thousand Oaks, CA: Corwin Press.

Strickland, Dorothy S., and Judith A. Schickedanz. 2009. *Learning About Print in Preschool*, 2nd ed. International Reading Association: Newark, DE.

Tompkins, Gail E. 2010. *Literacy for the 21st Century: A Balanced Approach*, 5th ed. Boston, MA: Pearson.

Index

Index